INDEX

Using the <del> and <ins> elements for strikethrough and underline

Using the <q> element for short inline quotations

Creating a login form with username and password fields

Creating a registration form with validation

Creating a contact form with email validation

Creating a feedback form with textarea

Embedding Google Maps with iframes

Using the <address> element for contact information

Creating a responsive layout using media queries

Using the <article> and <section> elements for structuring content

Using the <aside> element for sidebars

Creating a footer with copyright information

Using the <header> element for page headers

Creating dropdown menus with CSS

Using the <fieldset> and <legend> elements for grouping form controls

Creating a slideshow with images

Creating an accordion-style FAQ section

Using the <datalist> element for autocomplete

Creating a sitemap for a website

Using the <nav> element for navigation links

Using the <time> element for dates and times

Using the <mark> element for highlighting text

Creating tooltips using the title attribute

Creating a photo gallery with thumbnails

Using the <figure> and <figcaption> elements for image captions

Creating a dropdown navigation menu with hover effects

Using the <meter> element for displaying a gauge

Using the <progress> element for showing progress bars

Creating a responsive image grid

Using the <details> and <summary> elements for collapsible content

Creating a timeline using lists and CSS

Implementing CSS transitions for hover effects

Using the <canvas> element for drawing graphics

Creating a basic SVG graphic and embedding it in XHTML

Implementing a simple JavaScript slideshow with XHTML

Creating a popup modal with CSS and XHTML

Implementing a tabbed navigation interface

Creating a sticky/fixed header or sidebar

Implementing a simple lightbox effect for images

Creating a multi-column layout using CSS and XHTML

Implementing smooth scrolling to anchor links

Using CSS grid for layout

Using CSS flexbox for layout

Implementing a dropdown mega menu

Creating a responsive navigation menu with a hamburger icon

Using CSS animations for interactive elements

Implementing form validation using JavaScript and XHTML

Creating a countdown timer using JavaScript and XHTML

Implementing a character counter for textarea inputs

Creating a responsive carousel/slider

Using XHTML data attributes for storing extra information

Implementing a "load more" button for dynamic content

Creating a sticky footer that stays at the bottom of the page

Implementing parallax scrolling effects

Creating a 404 error page with a custom design

Implementing lazy loading for images

Using XHTML for accessibility enhancements (ARIA attributes)

Implementing a back-to-top button with smooth scrolling

Creating a newsletter signup form with validation

Implementing a search bar with autocomplete suggestions

Using XHTML for internationalization (language attributes)

Implementing a cookie consent banner

Creating a responsive pricing table

Using XHTML for semantic markup (semantic elements)

Implementing a hover effect with image overlays

Creating a progress indicator for form submission

Implementing a "read more" button for expanding text

Using XHTML for SEO optimization (meta tags, structured data)

Implementing drag-and-drop functionality

Creating a sidebar navigation menu with collapsible sections

Using XHTML for responsive typography (viewport units, fluid typography)

Implementing keyboard navigation for accessibility

Creating a mockup webpage based on a given design brief

Creating a Basic XHTML Document

```
<!DOCTYPE html PUBLIC "-//W3C//DTD XHTML 1.0 Strict//EN"
    "http://www.w3.org/TR/xhtml1/DTD/xhtml1-strict.dtd">
<html xmlns="http://www.w3.org/1999/xhtml" xml:lang="en" lang="en">
<head>
  <title>Basic XHTML Document</title>
  <meta http-equiv="Content-Type" content="text/html; charset=utf-8" />
</head>
<body>


</body>
</html>
```

Adding Headings and Paragraphs

```
<!DOCTYPE html PUBLIC "-//W3C//DTD XHTML 1.0 Strict//EN"
    "http://www.w3.org/TR/xhtml1/DTD/xhtml1-strict.dtd">
<html xmlns="http://www.w3.org/1999/xhtml" xml:lang="en" lang="en">
<head>
  <title>Adding Headings and Paragraphs</title>
  <meta http-equiv="Content-Type" content="text/html; charset=utf-8" />
</head>
<body>
<h1>Main Heading</h1>
<p>This is a paragraph of text. It demonstrates how paragraphs are structured in
XHTML.</p>
<h2>Subheading 1</h2>
<p>This is another paragraph.</p>
</body>
</html>
```

Inserting Line Breaks and Horizontal Rules

```
<!DOCTYPE html PUBLIC "-//W3C//DTD XHTML 1.0 Strict//EN"
    "http://www.w3.org/TR/xhtml1/DTD/xhtml1-strict.dtd">
<html xmlns="http://www.w3.org/1999/xhtml" xml:lang="en" lang="en">
<head>
  <title>Inserting Line Breaks and Horizontal Rules</title>
  <meta http-equiv="Content-Type" content="text/html; charset=utf-8" />
</head>
<body>
<p>This is a paragraph with a line break.<br />
This text appears on a new line.</p>
<hr />
<p>This paragraph is separated by a horizontal rule.</p>
</body>
</html>
```

Using Lists (Ordered and Unordered)

```
<!DOCTYPE html PUBLIC "-//W3C//DTD XHTML 1.0 Strict//EN"
    "http://www.w3.org/TR/xhtml1/DTD/xhtml1-strict.dtd">
<html xmlns="http://www.w3.org/1999/xhtml" xml:lang="en" lang="en">
<head>
  <title>Using Lists (Ordered and Unordered)</title>
  <meta http-equiv="Content-Type" content="text/html; charset=utf-8" />
</head>
<body>
<h2>Unordered List Example</h2>
<ul>
  <li>Item 1</li>
```

```
  <li>Item 2</li>
  <li>Item 3</li>
</ul>
<h2>Ordered List Example</h2>
<ol>
  <li>Step 1</li>
  <li>Step 2</li>
  <li>Step 3</li>
</ol>
</body>
</html>
```

Formatting Text (Bold, Italic, Underline)

```
<!DOCTYPE html PUBLIC "-//W3C//DTD XHTML 1.0 Strict//EN"
    "http://www.w3.org/TR/xhtml1/DTD/xhtml1-strict.dtd">
<html xmlns="http://www.w3.org/1999/xhtml" xml:lang="en" lang="en">
<head>
  <title>Formatting Text (Bold, Italic, Underline)</title>
  <meta http-equiv="Content-Type" content="text/html; charset=utf-8" />
</head>
<body>
<p>This paragraph contains <strong>bold text</strong>, <em>italic text</em>,
and <u>underlined text</u>.</p>
</body>
</html>
```

Adding Images and Setting Attributes

```
<!DOCTYPE html PUBLIC "-//W3C//DTD XHTML 1.0 Strict//EN"
```

```
    "http://www.w3.org/TR/xhtml1/DTD/xhtml1-strict.dtd">
<html xmlns="http://www.w3.org/1999/xhtml" xml:lang="en" lang="en">
<head>
   <title>Adding Images and Setting Attributes</title>
   <meta http-equiv="Content-Type" content="text/html; charset=utf-8" />
</head>
<body>
<h1>Adding Images and Setting Attributes</h1>
<p>Example of adding an image with XHTML:</p>
<img src="image.jpg" alt="Description of the image" width="300" height="200"
/>
</body>
</html>
```

Creating Hyperlinks to External Websites

```
<!DOCTYPE html PUBLIC "-//W3C//DTD XHTML 1.0 Strict//EN"
    "http://www.w3.org/TR/xhtml1/DTD/xhtml1-strict.dtd">
<html xmlns="http://www.w3.org/1999/xhtml" xml:lang="en" lang="en">
<head>
   <title>Creating Hyperlinks to External Websites</title>
   <meta http-equiv="Content-Type" content="text/html; charset=utf-8" />
</head>
<body>
<h1>Creating Hyperlinks to External Websites</h1>
<p>Example of creating a hyperlink to an external website:</p>
<a href="https://www.example.com" target="_blank">Visit Example
Website</a>
</body> </html>
```

Creating Hyperlinks to Local Pages Within the Site

```
<!DOCTYPE html PUBLIC "-//W3C//DTD XHTML 1.0 Strict//EN"
    "http://www.w3.org/TR/xhtml1/DTD/xhtml1-strict.dtd">
<html xmlns="http://www.w3.org/1999/xhtml" xml:lang="en" lang="en">
<head>
  <title>Creating Hyperlinks to Local Pages Within the Site</title>
  <meta http-equiv="Content-Type" content="text/html; charset=utf-8" />
</head>
<body>
<h1>Creating Hyperlinks to Local Pages Within the Site</h1>
<p>Example of creating hyperlinks to local pages:</p>
<ul>
  <li><a href="page1.xhtml">Page 1</a></li>
  <li><a href="page2.xhtml">Page 2</a></li>
  <li><a href="subfolder/page3.xhtml">Page 3 in Subfolder</a></li>
</ul>
</body>
</html>
```

Creating Tables with Rows and Columns

```
<!DOCTYPE html PUBLIC "-//W3C//DTD XHTML 1.0 Strict//EN"
    "http://www.w3.org/TR/xhtml1/DTD/xhtml1-strict.dtd">
<html xmlns="http://www.w3.org/1999/xhtml" xml:lang="en" lang="en">
<head>
  <title>Creating Tables with Rows and Columns</title>
  <meta http-equiv="Content-Type" content="text/html; charset=utf-8" />
</head>
<body>
```

```
<h1>Creating Tables with Rows and Columns</h1>
<table border="1">
   <caption>Sample Table</caption>
   <tr>
     <th>Header 1</th>
     <th>Header 2</th>
     <th>Header 3</th>
   </tr>
   <tr>
     <td>Row 1, Cell 1</td>
     <td>Row 1, Cell 2</td>
     <td>Row 1, Cell 3</td>
   </tr>
   <tr>
     <td>Row 2, Cell 1</td>
     <td>Row 2, Cell 2</td>
     <td>Row 2, Cell 3</td>
   </tr>
</table>
</body>
</html>
```

Applying Styles with Inline CSS

```
<!DOCTYPE html PUBLIC "-//W3C//DTD XHTML 1.0 Strict//EN"
     "http://www.w3.org/TR/xhtml1/DTD/xhtml1-strict.dtd">
<html xmlns="http://www.w3.org/1999/xhtml" xml:lang="en" lang="en">
<head>
   <title>Applying Styles with Inline CSS</title>
```

```
  <meta http-equiv="Content-Type" content="text/html; charset=utf-8" />
</head>
<body>
<h1 style="color: blue; text-align: center;">Heading with Inline CSS</h1>
<p style="font-size: 16px; font-family: Arial, sans-serif;">Paragraph with inline styles.</p>
</body>
</html>
```

Applying Styles with Internal CSS

```
<!DOCTYPE html PUBLIC "-//W3C//DTD XHTML 1.0 Strict//EN"
      "http://www.w3.org/TR/xhtml1/DTD/xhtml1-strict.dtd">
<html xmlns="http://www.w3.org/1999/xhtml" xml:lang="en" lang="en">
<head>
  <title>Applying Styles with Internal CSS</title>
  <meta http-equiv="Content-Type" content="text/html; charset=utf-8" />
  <style type="text/css">
    h1 {
      color: green;
      text-align: center;
    }
    p {
      font-size: 18px;
      font-family: Verdana, sans-serif;
    }
  </style>
</head>
<body>
```

```
<h1>Heading with Internal CSS</h1>
<p>Paragraph with internal styles.</p>
</body>
</html>
```

Applying Styles with External CSS

Create a file named styles.css with the following content:

```css
/* styles.css */
h1 {
    color: red;
    text-align: center;
}
p {
    font-size: 20px;
    font-family: "Times New Roman", serif;
}
```

And reference this external CSS file in your XHTML document:

```
<!DOCTYPE html PUBLIC "-//W3C//DTD XHTML 1.0 Strict//EN"
        "http://www.w3.org/TR/xhtml1/DTD/xhtml1-strict.dtd">
<html xmlns="http://www.w3.org/1999/xhtml" xml:lang="en" lang="en">
<head>
    <title>Applying Styles with External CSS</title>
    <meta http-equiv="Content-Type" content="text/html; charset=utf-8" />
    <link rel="stylesheet" type="text/css" href="styles.css" />
</head>
<body>
```

```
<h1>Heading with External CSS</h1>

<p>Paragraph with external styles.</p>

</body>

</html>
```

Creating Forms with Text Inputs

```
<!DOCTYPE html PUBLIC "-//W3C//DTD XHTML 1.0 Strict//EN"

    "http://www.w3.org/TR/xhtml1/DTD/xhtml1-strict.dtd">

<html xmlns="http://www.w3.org/1999/xhtml" xml:lang="en" lang="en">

<head>

  <title>Creating Forms with Text Inputs</title>

  <meta http-equiv="Content-Type" content="text/html; charset=utf-8" />

</head>

<body>

<form action="#" method="post">

  <label for="username">Username:</label>

  <input type="text" id="username" name="username" /><br />

  <label for="password">Password:</label>

  <input type="password" id="password" name="password" /><br />

  <input type="submit" value="Submit" />

  <input type="reset" value="Reset" />

</form>

</body>

</html>
```

Creating Forms with Radio Buttons and Checkboxes

```
<!DOCTYPE html PUBLIC "-//W3C//DTD XHTML 1.0 Strict//EN"

    "http://www.w3.org/TR/xhtml1/DTD/xhtml1-strict.dtd">
```

```
<html xmlns="http://www.w3.org/1999/xhtml" xml:lang="en" lang="en">
<head>
   <title>Creating Forms with Radio Buttons and Checkboxes</title>
   <meta http-equiv="Content-Type" content="text/html; charset=utf-8" />
</head>
<body>
<form action="#" method="post">
   <p>Choose your gender:</p>
   <input type="radio" id="male" name="gender" value="male" />
   <label for="male">Male</label><br />
   <input type="radio" id="female" name="gender" value="female" />
   <label for="female">Female</label><br />
   <input type="radio" id="other" name="gender" value="other" />
   <label for="other">Other</label><br />
   <p>Choose your interests:</p>
   <input type="checkbox" id="sport" name="interest" value="sport" />
   <label for="sport">Sport</label><br />
   <input type="checkbox" id="music" name="interest" value="music" />
   <label for="music">Music</label><br />
   <input type="checkbox" id="reading" name="interest" value="reading" />
   <label for="reading">Reading</label><br />
   <input type="submit" value="Submit" />
   <input type="reset" value="Reset" />
 </form>
 </body>
 </html>
```

Creating Forms with Select Menus

```
<!DOCTYPE html PUBLIC "-//W3C//DTD XHTML 1.0 Strict//EN"
     "http://www.w3.org/TR/xhtml1/DTD/xhtml1-strict.dtd">
<html xmlns="http://www.w3.org/1999/xhtml" xml:lang="en" lang="en">
<head>
   <title>Creating Forms with Select Menus</title>
   <meta http-equiv="Content-Type" content="text/html; charset=utf-8" />
</head>
<body>
<form action="#" method="post">
   <label for="country">Choose your country:</label>
   <select id="country" name="country">
     <option value="usa">USA</option>
     <option value="uk">UK</option>
     <option value="canada">Canada</option>
     <option value="australia">Australia</option>
   </select><br />
   <label for="city">Choose your city:</label>
   <select id="city" name="city">
     <option value="ny">New York</option>
     <option value="london">London</option>
     <option value="toronto">Toronto</option>
     <option value="sydney">Sydney</option>
   </select><br />
   <input type="submit" value="Submit" />
   <input type="reset" value="Reset" />
</form>
</body></html>
```

Creating Forms with Submit and Reset Buttons

```
<!DOCTYPE html PUBLIC "-//W3C//DTD XHTML 1.0 Strict//EN"
    "http://www.w3.org/TR/xhtml1/DTD/xhtml1-strict.dtd">
<html xmlns="http://www.w3.org/1999/xhtml" xml:lang="en" lang="en">
<head>
  <title>Creating Forms with Submit and Reset Buttons</title>
  <meta http-equiv="Content-Type" content="text/html; charset=utf-8" />
</head>
<body>
<form action="#" method="post">
  <label for="name">Name:</label>
  <input type="text" id="name" name="name" /><br />
  <label for="email">Email:</label>
  <input type="email" id="email" name="email" /><br />
  <input type="submit" value="Submit" />
  <input type="reset" value="Reset" />
</form>
</body>
</html>
```

Validating Forms Using XHTML Attributes

```
<!DOCTYPE html PUBLIC "-//W3C//DTD XHTML 1.0 Strict//EN"
    "http://www.w3.org/TR/xhtml1/DTD/xhtml1-strict.dtd">
<html xmlns="http://www.w3.org/1999/xhtml" xml:lang="en" lang="en">
<head>
  <title>Validating Forms Using XHTML Attributes</title>
  <meta http-equiv="Content-Type" content="text/html; charset=utf-8" />
</head>
```

```
<body>

<form action="#" method="post">

   <label for="username">Username:</label>

   <input type="text" id="username" name="username" required /><br />

   <label for="password">Password:</label>

   <input type="password" id="password" name="password" required /><br />

   <input type="submit" value="Submit" />

   <input type="reset" value="Reset" />

</form>

</body>

</html>
```

Embedding Audio Files

```
<!DOCTYPE html PUBLIC "-//W3C//DTD XHTML 1.0 Strict//EN"

     "http://www.w3.org/TR/xhtml1/DTD/xhtml1-strict.dtd">

<html xmlns="http://www.w3.org/1999/xhtml" xml:lang="en" lang="en">

<head>

   <title>Embedding Audio Files</title>

   <meta http-equiv="Content-Type" content="text/html; charset=utf-8" />

</head>

<body>

<audio controls>

   <source src="audio-file.mp3" type="audio/mpeg" />

   Your browser does not support the audio element.

</audio>

</body>

</html>
```

Embedding Video Files

```
<!DOCTYPE html PUBLIC "-//W3C//DTD XHTML 1.0 Strict//EN"
    "http://www.w3.org/TR/xhtml1/DTD/xhtml1-strict.dtd">
<html xmlns="http://www.w3.org/1999/xhtml" xml:lang="en" lang="en">
<head>
  <title>Embedding Video Files</title>
  <meta http-equiv="Content-Type" content="text/html; charset=utf-8" />
</head>
<body>
<video controls width="400" height="300">
  <source src="video-file.mp4" type="video/mp4" />
  Your browser does not support the video element.
</video>
</body>
</html>
```

Using iframes to Embed External Content

```
<!DOCTYPE html PUBLIC "-//W3C//DTD XHTML 1.0 Strict//EN"
    "http://www.w3.org/TR/xhtml1/DTD/xhtml1-strict.dtd">
<html xmlns="http://www.w3.org/1999/xhtml" xml:lang="en" lang="en">
<head>
  <title>Using iframes to Embed External Content</title>
  <meta http-equiv="Content-Type" content="text/html; charset=utf-8" />
</head>
<body>
<h1>Embedding External Content with iframes</h1>
<iframe src="https://www.example.com" width="600" height="400"
frameborder="0">
```

```
    Your browser does not support iframes.

</iframe>

</body>

</html>
```

Using Meta Tags for SEO Purposes

```
<!DOCTYPE html PUBLIC "-//W3C//DTD XHTML 1.0 Strict//EN"

    "http://www.w3.org/TR/xhtml1/DTD/xhtml1-strict.dtd">

<html xmlns="http://www.w3.org/1999/xhtml" xml:lang="en" lang="en">

<head>

    <title>Using Meta Tags for SEO Purposes</title>

    <meta http-equiv="Content-Type" content="text/html; charset=utf-8" />

    <meta name="description" content="This is an example of using meta tags for

SEO purposes." />

    <meta name="keywords" content="XHTML, meta tags, SEO, example" />

    <meta name="author" content="Author Name" />

</head>

<body>

<h1>Using Meta Tags for SEO Purposes</h1>

<p>This document contains meta tags for SEO purposes.</p>

</body>

</html>
```

Creating a Simple Navigation Menu

```
<!DOCTYPE html PUBLIC "-//W3C//DTD XHTML 1.0 Strict//EN"

    "http://www.w3.org/TR/xhtml1/DTD/xhtml1-strict.dtd">

<html xmlns="http://www.w3.org/1999/xhtml" xml:lang="en" lang="en">

<head>
```

```
    <title>Creating a Simple Navigation Menu</title>
    <meta http-equiv="Content-Type" content="text/html; charset=utf-8" />
    <style type="text/css">
        ul.nav {
            list-style-type: none;
            margin: 0;
            padding: 0;
            overflow: hidden;
            background-color: #333;
        }
        ul.nav li {
            float: left;
        }
        ul.nav li a {
            display: block;
            color: white;
            text-align: center;
            padding: 14px 16px;
            text-decoration: none;
        }
        ul.nav li a:hover {
            background-color: #111;
        }
    </style>
</head>
<body>
<h1>Simple Navigation Menu</h1>
```

```
<ul class="nav">

  <li><a href="#home">Home</a></li>

  <li><a href="#about">About</a></li>

  <li><a href="#services">Services</a></li>

  <li><a href="#contact">Contact</a></li>

</ul>

</body>

</html>
```

Using the <div> and <span> Elements

```
<!DOCTYPE html PUBLIC "-//W3C//DTD XHTML 1.0 Strict//EN"

    "http://www.w3.org/TR/xhtml1/DTD/xhtml1-strict.dtd">

<html xmlns="http://www.w3.org/1999/xhtml" xml:lang="en" lang="en">

<head>

  <title>Using the &lt;div&gt; and &lt;span&gt; Elements</title>

  <meta http-equiv="Content-Type" content="text/html; charset=utf-8" />

  <style type="text/css">

    .container {

      border: 1px solid #000;

      padding: 10px;

    }

    .highlight {

      color: red;

    }

  </style>

</head>

<body>

<h1>Using the &lt;div&gt; and &lt;span&gt; Elements</h1>
```

```
<div class="container">

    <p>This is a paragraph inside a div container.</p>

    <p>This is another paragraph with a <span class="highlight">highlighted
text</span> inside a div container.</p>

</div>

</body>

</html>
```

Creating Ordered Lists with Different Types of Markers

```
<!DOCTYPE html PUBLIC "-//W3C//DTD XHTML 1.0 Strict//EN"
       "http://www.w3.org/TR/xhtml1/DTD/xhtml1-strict.dtd">
<html xmlns="http://www.w3.org/1999/xhtml" xml:lang="en" lang="en">
<head>
    <title>Creating Ordered Lists with Different Types of Markers</title>
    <meta http-equiv="Content-Type" content="text/html; charset=utf-8" />
</head>
<body>
<h1>Ordered Lists with Different Types of Markers</h1>
<ol type="1">
    <li>Item 1</li>
    <li>Item 2</li>
    <li>Item 3</li>
</ol>
<ol type="A">
    <li>Item A</li>
    <li>Item B</li>
    <li>Item C</li>
</ol>
```

```
<ol type="a">

  <li>Item a</li>

  <li>Item b</li>

  <li>Item c</li>

</ol>

<ol type="I">

  <li>Item I</li>

  <li>Item II</li>

  <li>Item III</li>

</ol>

<ol type="i">

  <li>Item i</li>

  <li>Item ii</li>

  <li>Item iii</li>

</ol>

</body>

</html>
```

Using the <abbr> and <acronym> Elements

```
<!DOCTYPE html PUBLIC "-//W3C//DTD XHTML 1.0 Strict//EN"

    "http://www.w3.org/TR/xhtml1/DTD/xhtml1-strict.dtd">

<html xmlns="http://www.w3.org/1999/xhtml" xml:lang="en" lang="en">

<head>

  <title>Using the &lt;abbr&gt; and &lt;acronym&gt; Elements</title>

  <meta http-equiv="Content-Type" content="text/html; charset=utf-8" />

</head>

<body>

<h1>Using the &lt;abbr&gt; and &lt;acronym&gt; Elements</h1>
```

```
<p>This is an example of an abbreviation: <abbr title="World Wide
Web">WWW</abbr>.</p>
<p>This is an example of an acronym: <acronym title="As Soon As
Possible">ASAP</acronym>.</p>
</body>
</html>
```

Using the <blockquote> Element for Quotations

```
<!DOCTYPE html PUBLIC "-//W3C//DTD XHTML 1.0 Strict//EN"
    "http://www.w3.org/TR/xhtml1/DTD/xhtml1-strict.dtd">
<html xmlns="http://www.w3.org/1999/xhtml" xml:lang="en" lang="en">
<head>
   <title>Using the &lt;blockquote&gt; Element for Quotations</title>
   <meta http-equiv="Content-Type" content="text/html; charset=utf-8" />
</head>
<body>
<h1>Using the &lt;blockquote&gt; Element for Quotations</h1>
<blockquote cite="https://www.example.com">
   This is a long quotation that is set off from the main text using the blockquote
element. It can contain multiple lines and is typically styled differently from the
surrounding text.
</blockquote>
</body>
</html>
```

Using the <cite> Element for Citations

```
<!DOCTYPE html PUBLIC "-//W3C//DTD XHTML 1.0 Strict//EN"
    "http://www.w3.org/TR/xhtml1/DTD/xhtml1-strict.dtd">
```

```
<html xmlns="http://www.w3.org/1999/xhtml" xml:lang="en" lang="en">
<head>
   <title>Using the &lt;cite&gt; Element for Citations</title>
   <meta http-equiv="Content-Type" content="text/html; charset=utf-8" />
</head>
<body>
<h1>Using the &lt;cite&gt; Element for Citations</h1>
<p>This is an example of a citation: <cite>The Great Gatsby</cite> by F. Scott
Fitzgerald.</p>
</body>
</html>
```

Using the <del> and `<ins> Elements for Strikethrough and Underline

```
<!DOCTYPE html PUBLIC "-//W3C//DTD XHTML 1.0 Strict//EN"
    "http://www.w3.org/TR/xhtml1/DTD/xhtml1-strict.dtd">
<html xmlns="http://www.w3.org/1999/xhtml" xml:lang="en" lang="en">
<head>
   <title>Using the &lt;del&gt; and &lt;ins&gt; Elements for Strikethrough and
Underline</title>
   <meta http-equiv="Content-Type" content="text/html; charset=utf-8" />
</head>
<body>
<h1>Using the &lt;del&gt; and &lt;ins&gt; Elements for Strikethrough and
Underline</h1>
<p>This is an example of <del>deleted text</del> and <ins>inserted
text</ins>.</p>
</body> </html>
```

Using the <q> Element for Short Inline Quotations

```
<!DOCTYPE html PUBLIC "-//W3C//DTD XHTML 1.0 Strict//EN"
    "http://www.w3.org/TR/xhtml1/DTD/xhtml1-strict.dtd">
<html xmlns="http://www.w3.org/1999/xhtml" xml:lang="en" lang="en">
<head>
   <title>Using the &lt;q&gt; Element for Short Inline Quotations</title>
   <meta http-equiv="Content-Type" content="text/html; charset=utf-8" />
</head>
<body>
<h1>Using the &lt;q&gt; Element for Short Inline Quotations</h1>
<p>This is an example of a short inline quotation: <q>This is an inline
quotation.</q></p>
</body>
</html>
```

Creating a Login Form with Username and Password Fields

```
<!DOCTYPE html PUBLIC "-//W3C//DTD XHTML 1.0 Strict//EN"
    "http://www.w3.org/TR/xhtml1/DTD/xhtml1-strict.dtd">
<html xmlns="http://www.w3.org/1999/xhtml" xml:lang="en" lang="en">
<head>
   <title>Login Form</title>
   <meta http-equiv="Content-Type" content="text/html; charset=utf-8" />
</head>
<body>
<h1>Login Form</h1>
<form action="#" method="post">
   <label for="username">Username:</label>
   <input type="text" id="username" name="username" /><br />
```

```
  <label for="password">Password:</label>
  <input type="password" id="password" name="password" /><br />
  <input type="submit" value="Login" />
  <input type="reset" value="Reset" />
</form>
</body>
</html>
```

Creating a Registration Form with Validation

```
<!DOCTYPE html PUBLIC "-//W3C//DTD XHTML 1.0 Strict//EN"
    "http://www.w3.org/TR/xhtml1/DTD/xhtml1-strict.dtd">
<html xmlns="http://www.w3.org/1999/xhtml" xml:lang="en" lang="en">
<head>
  <title>Registration Form</title>
  <meta http-equiv="Content-Type" content="text/html; charset=utf-8" />
  <script type="text/javascript">
    function validateForm() {
      var username = document.getElementById('username').value;
      var password = document.getElementById('password').value;

      if (username === '' || password === '') {
        alert('Please fill in all fields.');
        return false;
      }

      return true;
    }
  </script>
```

```
</head>
<body>
<h1>Registration Form</h1>
<form action="#" method="post" onsubmit="return validateForm();">
   <label for="username">Username:</label>
   <input type="text" id="username" name="username" /><br />
   <label for="password">Password:</label>
   <input type="password" id="password" name="password" /><br />
   <input type="submit" value="Register" />
   <input type="reset" value="Reset" />
</form>
</body>
</html>
```

Creating a Contact Form with Email Validation

```
<!DOCTYPE html PUBLIC "-//W3C//DTD XHTML 1.0 Strict//EN"
     "http://www.w3.org/TR/xhtml1/DTD/xhtml1-strict.dtd">
<html xmlns="http://www.w3.org/1999/xhtml" xml:lang="en" lang="en">
<head>
   <title>Contact Form</title>
   <meta http-equiv="Content-Type" content="text/html; charset=utf-8" />
   <script type="text/javascript">
     function validateEmail() {
        var email = document.getElementById('email').value;
        var pattern = /^[^\s@]+@[^\s@]+\.[^\s@]+$/;
        return pattern.test(email);
     }
```

```
        function validateForm() {
            var name = document.getElementById('name').value;
            var email = document.getElementById('email').value;
            var message = document.getElementById('message').value;


            if (name === '' || email === '' || message === '') {
                alert('Please fill in all fields.');
                return false;
            }
            if (!validateEmail()) {
                alert('Please enter a valid email address.');
                return false;
            }
            return true;
        }
    </script>
</head>
<body>
<h1>Contact Form</h1>
<form action="#" method="post" onsubmit="return validateForm();">
    <label for="name">Name:</label>
    <input type="text" id="name" name="name" /><br />
    <label for="email">Email:</label>
    <input type="text" id="email" name="email" /><br />
    <label for="message">Message:</label><br />
    <textarea id="message" name="message" rows="5" cols="30"></textarea><br
/>
    <input type="submit" value="Submit" />
```

```
    <input type="reset" value="Reset" />
</form>
</body>
</html>
```

Creating a Feedback Form with Textarea

```
<!DOCTYPE html PUBLIC "-//W3C//DTD XHTML 1.0 Strict//EN"
     "http://www.w3.org/TR/xhtml1/DTD/xhtml1-strict.dtd">
<html xmlns="http://www.w3.org/1999/xhtml" xml:lang="en" lang="en">
<head>
   <title>Feedback Form</title>
   <meta http-equiv="Content-Type" content="text/html; charset=utf-8" />
</head>
<body>
<h1>Feedback Form</h1>
<form action="#" method="post">
   <label for="name">Name:</label>
   <input type="text" id="name" name="name" /><br />
   <label for="email">Email:</label>
   <input type="text" id="email" name="email" /><br />
   <label for="feedback">Feedback:</label><br />
   <textarea id="feedback" name="feedback" rows="5"
cols="30"></textarea><br />
   <input type="submit" value="Submit" />
   <input type="reset" value="Reset" />
</form>
</body>
</html>
```

Embedding Google Maps with iframes

```
<!DOCTYPE html PUBLIC "-//W3C//DTD XHTML 1.0 Strict//EN"
    "http://www.w3.org/TR/xhtml1/DTD/xhtml1-strict.dtd">
<html xmlns="http://www.w3.org/1999/xhtml" xml:lang="en" lang="en">
<head>
  <title>Embedding Google Maps</title>
  <meta http-equiv="Content-Type" content="text/html; charset=utf-8" />
</head>
<body>
<h1>Embedding Google Maps</h1>
<iframe
src="https://www.google.com/maps/embed?pb=!1m18!1m12!1m3!1d387109.90
650794835!2d-
74.2598725!3d40.6975898!2m3!1f0!2f0!3f0!3m2!1i1024!2i768!4f13.1!3m3!1m
2!1s0x89c24fa5d33f083b%3A0xc80b8f06e177fe62!2sNew%20York%2C%20N
Y%2C%20USA!5e0!3m2!1sen!2sin!4v1592242350074!5m2!1sen!2sin"
width="600" height="450" frameborder="0" style="border:0;"
allowfullscreen="" aria-hidden="false" tabindex="0"></iframe>
</body>
</html>
```

Using the <address> Element for Contact Information

```
<!DOCTYPE html PUBLIC "-//W3C//DTD XHTML 1.0 Strict//EN"
    "http://www.w3.org/TR/xhtml1/DTD/xhtml1-strict.dtd">
<html xmlns="http://www.w3.org/1999/xhtml" xml:lang="en" lang="en">
<head>
  <title>Contact Information</title>
  <meta http-equiv="Content-Type" content="text/html; charset=utf-8" />
```

```
</head>

<body>

<h1>Contact Information</h1>

<address>

  <strong>John Doe</strong><br />

  Email: <a

href="mailto:john.doe@example.com">john.doe@example.com</a><br />

  Phone: +1234567890<br />

  Address: 123 Main St, Cityville, State, Country

</address>

</body>

</html>
```

Creating a Responsive Layout Using Media Queries

```
<!DOCTYPE html PUBLIC "-//W3C//DTD XHTML 1.0 Strict//EN"
    "http://www.w3.org/TR/xhtml1/DTD/xhtml1-strict.dtd">
<html xmlns="http://www.w3.org/1999/xhtml" xml:lang="en" lang="en">
<head>

  <title>Responsive Layout</title>

  <meta http-equiv="Content-Type" content="text/html; charset=utf-8" />

  <style type="text/css">

    body {

      font-family: Arial, sans-serif;

      margin: 0;

      padding: 0;

    }

    .container {

      width: 80%;
```

```
      margin: 0 auto;

      padding: 20px;

      background-color: #f0f0f0;

    }

    @media screen and (max-width: 600px) {

      .container {

        width: 100%;

        padding: 10px;

      }

    }

  </style>

</head>

<body>

<div class="container">

  <h1>Responsive Layout</h1>

  <p>This is a responsive layout example.</p>

</div>

</body>

</html>
```

Using the <article> and <section> Elements for Structuring Content

```
<!DOCTYPE html PUBLIC "-//W3C//DTD XHTML 1.0 Strict//EN"

    "http://www.w3.org/TR/xhtml1/DTD/xhtml1-strict.dtd">

<html xmlns="http://www.w3.org/1999/xhtml" xml:lang="en" lang="en">

<head>

  <title>Structured Content with Article and Section</title>

  <meta http-equiv="Content-Type" content="text/html; charset=utf-8" />

</head>
```

```
<body>
<article>
  <h1>Main Article</h1>
  <section>
    <h2>Section 1</h2>
    <p>This is the content of section 1.</p>
  </section>
  <section>
    <h2>Section 2</h2>
    <p>This is the content of section 2.</p>
  </section>
</article>
</body>
</html>
```

Using the <aside> Element for Sidebars

```
<!DOCTYPE html PUBLIC "-//W3C//DTD XHTML 1.0 Strict//EN"
    "http://www.w3.org/TR/xhtml1/DTD/xhtml1-strict.dtd">
<html xmlns="http://www.w3.org/1999/xhtml" xml:lang="en" lang="en">
<head>
  <title>Using the &lt;aside&gt; Element for Sidebar</title>
  <meta http-equiv="Content-Type" content="text/html; charset=utf-8" />
  <style type="text/css">
    .sidebar {
      float: right;
      width: 30%;
      background-color: #f0f0f0;
      padding: 10px;
```

```
      margin-left: 10px;
    }
  </style>
</head>
<body>
<article>
  <h1>Main Content</h1>
  <p>This is the main content area.</p>
</article>
<aside class="sidebar">
  <h2>Sidebar</h2>
  <p>This is the sidebar content.</p>
</aside>
</body>
</html>
```

Creating a Footer with Copyright Information

```
<!DOCTYPE html PUBLIC "-//W3C//DTD XHTML 1.0 Strict//EN"
      "http://www.w3.org/TR/xhtml1/DTD/xhtml1-strict.dtd">
<html xmlns="http://www.w3.org/1999/xhtml" xml:lang="en" lang="en">
<head>
  <title>Footer with Copyright Information</title>
  <meta http-equiv="Content-Type" content="text/html; charset=utf-8" />
  <style type="text/css">
    footer {
      text-align: center;
      padding: 10px;
      background-color: #333;
```

```
color: #fff;

position: absolute;

bottom: 0;

width: 100%;

}

</style>

</head>

<body>

<footer>

<p>&copy; 2024 Your Website Name. All rights reserved.</p>

</footer>

</body>

</html>
```

Using the <header> Element for Page Headers

```
<!DOCTYPE html PUBLIC "-//W3C//DTD XHTML 1.0 Strict//EN"

    "http://www.w3.org/TR/xhtml11/DTD/xhtml11-strict.dtd">

<html xmlns="http://www.w3.org/1999/xhtml" xml:lang="en" lang="en">

<head>

  <title>Using the &lt;header&gt; Element for Page Headers</title>

  <meta http-equiv="Content-Type" content="text/html; charset=utf-8" />

  <style type="text/css">

    header {

        background-color: #333;

        color: #fff;

        padding: 10px;

        text-align: center;

    }
```

```
    </style>
</head>
<body>
<header>
    <h1>Welcome to Our Website</h1>
    <p>Explore and Discover</p>
</header>
<p>Main content of the page goes here...</p>
</body>
</html>
```

Creating Dropdown Menus with CSS

```
<!DOCTYPE html PUBLIC "-//W3C//DTD XHTML 1.0 Strict//EN"
    "http://www.w3.org/TR/xhtml1/DTD/xhtml1-strict.dtd">
<html xmlns="http://www.w3.org/1999/xhtml" xml:lang="en" lang="en">
<head>
    <title>Dropdown Menu with CSS</title>
    <meta http-equiv="Content-Type" content="text/html; charset=utf-8" />
    <style type="text/css">
        .dropdown {
            position: relative;
            display: inline-block;
        }
        .dropdown-content {
            display: none;
            position: absolute;
            background-color: #f9f9f9;
            min-width: 160px;
```

```
    box-shadow: 0px 8px 16px 0px rgba(0,0,0,0.2);
    z-index: 1;
  }
  .dropdown:hover .dropdown-content {
    display: block;
  }
  .dropdown-content a {
    color: black;
    padding: 12px 16px;
    text-decoration: none;
    display: block;
  }
  .dropdown-content a:hover {background-color: #f1f1f1}
  </style>
</head>
<body>
<div class="dropdown">
  <span>Hover over me</span>
  <div class="dropdown-content">
    <a href="#">Link 1</a>
    <a href="#">Link 2</a>
    <a href="#">Link 3</a>
  </div>
</div>
</body>
</html>
```

Using the <fieldset> and <legend> Elements for Grouping Form Controls

```
<!DOCTYPE html PUBLIC "-//W3C//DTD XHTML 1.0 Strict//EN"
    "http://www.w3.org/TR/xhtml1/DTD/xhtml1-strict.dtd">
<html xmlns="http://www.w3.org/1999/xhtml" xml:lang="en" lang="en">
<head>
  <title>Using the &lt;fieldset&gt; and &lt;legend&gt; Elements for Grouping
Form Controls</title>
  <meta http-equiv="Content-Type" content="text/html; charset=utf-8" />
</head>
<body>
<form action="#" method="post">
  <fieldset>
    <legend>Personal Information</legend>
    <label for="name">Name:</label>
    <input type="text" id="name" name="name" /><br />
    <label for="email">Email:</label>
    <input type="text" id="email" name="email" /><br />
    <label for="phone">Phone:</label>
    <input type="text" id="phone" name="phone" /><br />
  </fieldset>
    <fieldset>
    <legend>Address Information</legend>
      <label for="address">Address:</label>
    <input type="text" id="address" name="address" /><br />
      <label for="city">City:</label>
    <input type="text" id="city" name="city" /><br />
      <label for="zipcode">Zip Code:</label>
    <input type="text" id="zipcode" name="zipcode" /><br />
```

```
    </fieldset>
      <input type="submit" value="Submit" />
    <input type="reset" value="Reset" />
</form>
</body>
</html>
```

Creating a Slideshow with Images

```
<!DOCTYPE html PUBLIC "-//W3C//DTD XHTML 1.0 Strict//EN"
      "http://www.w3.org/TR/xhtml1/DTD/xhtml1-strict.dtd">
<html xmlns="http://www.w3.org/1999/xhtml" xml:lang="en" lang="en">
<head>
  <title>Slideshow with Images</title>
  <meta http-equiv="Content-Type" content="text/html; charset=utf-8" />
  <style type="text/css">
    .slideshow-container {
      max-width: 600px;
      position: relative;
      margin: auto;
    }
    .mySlides {
      display: none;
    }
    .prev, .next {
      cursor: pointer;
      position: absolute;
      top: 50%;
      width: auto;
```

```
      padding: 16px;
      margin-top: -22px;
      color: white;
      font-weight: bold;
      font-size: 18px;
      transition: 0.6s ease;
      border-radius: 0 3px 3px 0;
      user-select: none;
    }
    .next {
      right: 0;
      border-radius: 3px 0 0 3px;
    }
    .prev:hover, .next:hover {
      background-color: rgba(0, 0, 0, 0.8);
    }
  </style>
</head>
<body>
<div class="slideshow-container">
  <div class="mySlides">
    <img src="slide1.jpg" style="width:100%">
  </div>
  <div class="mySlides">
    <img src="slide2.jpg" style="width:100%">
  </div>
  <div class="mySlides">
    <img src="slide3.jpg" style="width:100%">
```

```
    </div>
    <a class="prev" onclick="plusSlides(-1)">&#10094;</a>
    <a class="next" onclick="plusSlides(1)">&#10095;</a>
</div>
<script>
    var slideIndex = 1;
    showSlides(slideIndex);
    function plusSlides(n) {
        showSlides(slideIndex += n);
    }
    function showSlides(n) {
        var i;
        var slides = document.getElementsByClassName("mySlides");
        if (n > slides.length) {slideIndex = 1}
        if (n < 1) {slideIndex = slides.length}
        for (i = 0; i < slides.length; i++) {
            slides[i].style.display = "none";
        }
        slides[slideIndex-1].style.display = "block";
    }
</script>
</body>
</html>
```

Creating an Accordion-Style FAQ Section

```
<!DOCTYPE html PUBLIC "-//W3C//DTD XHTML 1.0 Strict//EN"
        "http://www.w3.org/TR/xhtml1/DTD/xhtml1-strict.dtd">
<html xmlns="http://www.w3.org/1999/xhtml" xml:lang="en" lang="en">
```

```
<head>
  <title>Accordion-Style FAQ Section</title>
  <meta http-equiv="Content-Type" content="text/html; charset=utf-8" />
  <style type="text/css">
    .accordion {
      background-color: #f9f9f9;
      color: #333;
      cursor: pointer;
      padding: 18px;
      width: 100%;
      border: none;
      text-align: left;
      outline: none;
      font-size: 15px;
      transition: 0.4s;
    }
    .panel {
      padding: 0 18px;
      display: none;
      background-color: white;
      overflow: hidden;
    }
    .panel p {
      padding: 10px;
    }
  </style>
</head>
<body>
```

```
<h2>FAQ (Frequently Asked Questions)</h2>
<button class="accordion">Question 1?</button>
<div class="panel">
  <p>Answer 1.</p>
</div>
<button class="accordion">Question 2?</button>
<div class="panel">
  <p>Answer 2.</p>
</div>
<button class="accordion">Question 3?</button>
<div class="panel">
  <p>Answer 3.</p>
</div>
<script>
  var accordions = document.getElementsByClassName("accordion");
  var i;
  for (i = 0; i < accordions.length; i++) {
    accordions[i].addEventListener("click", function() {
      this.classList.toggle("active");
      var panel = this.nextElementSibling;
      if (panel.style.display === "block") {
        panel.style.display = "none";
      } else {
        panel.style.display = "block";
      }
    });
  }
</script>
```

```
</body>
</html>
```

Using the <datalist> Element for Autocomplete

```
<!DOCTYPE html PUBLIC "-//W3C//DTD XHTML 1.0 Strict//EN"
      "http://www.w3.org/TR/xhtml1/DTD/xhtml1-strict.dtd">
<html xmlns="http://www.w3.org/1999/xhtml" xml:lang="en" lang="en">
<head>
   <title>Using the &lt;datalist&gt; Element for Autocomplete</title>
   <meta http-equiv="Content-Type" content="text/html; charset=utf-8" />
</head>
<body>
<h1>Search Using Datalist</h1>
<form action="#" method="get">
   <label for="search">Search:</label>
   <input list="searchOptions" id="search" name="search" />
   <datalist id="searchOptions">
     <option value="HTML" />
     <option value="CSS" />
     <option value="JavaScript" />
     <option value="XHTML" />
     <option value="XML" />
     <option value="JSON" />
   </datalist>
   <input type="submit" value="Search" />
</form>
</body>
</html>
```

Creating a Sitemap for a Website

```
<!DOCTYPE html PUBLIC "-//W3C//DTD XHTML 1.0 Strict//EN"
    "http://www.w3.org/TR/xhtml1/DTD/xhtml1-strict.dtd">
<html xmlns="http://www.w3.org/1999/xhtml" xml:lang="en" lang="en">
<head>
  <title>Sitemap for a Website</title>
  <meta http-equiv="Content-Type" content="text/html; charset=utf-8" />
</head>
<body>
<nav>
  <ul>
    <li><a href="/">Home</a></li>
    <li><a href="/about">About Us</a></li>
    <li><a href="/services">Services</a></li>
    <li><a href="/products">Products</a></li>
    <li><a href="/contact">Contact Us</a></li>
  </ul>
</nav>
</body>
</html>
```

Using the <nav> Element for Navigation Links

```
<!DOCTYPE html PUBLIC "-//W3C//DTD XHTML 1.0 Strict//EN"
    "http://www.w3.org/TR/xhtml1/DTD/xhtml1-strict.dtd">
<html xmlns="http://www.w3.org/1999/xhtml" xml:lang="en" lang="en">
<head>
  <title>Using the &lt;nav&gt; Element for Navigation Links</title>
  <meta http-equiv="Content-Type" content="text/html; charset=utf-8" />
```

```
</head>

<body>

<nav>

  <ul>

    <li><a href="/">Home</a></li>

    <li><a href="/about">About Us</a></li>

    <li><a href="/services">Services</a></li>

    <li><a href="/products">Products</a></li>

    <li><a href="/contact">Contact Us</a></li>

  </ul>

</nav>

</body>

</html>
```

Using the <time> Element for Dates and Times

```
<!DOCTYPE html PUBLIC "-//W3C//DTD XHTML 1.0 Strict//EN"

    "http://www.w3.org/TR/xhtml1/DTD/xhtml1-strict.dtd">

<html xmlns="http://www.w3.org/1999/xhtml" xml:lang="en" lang="en">

<head>

  <title>Using the &lt;time&gt; Element for Dates and Times</title>

  <meta http-equiv="Content-Type" content="text/html; charset=utf-8" />

</head>

<body>

<p>Article published on <time datetime="2024-06-15T10:30:00">June 15, 2024

at 10:30 AM</time>.</p>

</body>

</html>
```

Using the <mark> Element for Highlighting Text

```
<!DOCTYPE html PUBLIC "-//W3C//DTD XHTML 1.0 Strict//EN"
    "http://www.w3.org/TR/xhtml1/DTD/xhtml1-strict.dtd">
<html xmlns="http://www.w3.org/1999/xhtml" xml:lang="en" lang="en">
<head>
  <title>Using the &lt;mark&gt; Element for Highlighting Text</title>
  <meta http-equiv="Content-Type" content="text/html; charset=utf-8" />
</head>
<body>
<p>This is a <mark>highlighted</mark> text example.</p>
</body>
</html>
```

Creating Tooltips Using the title Attribute

```
<!DOCTYPE html PUBLIC "-//W3C//DTD XHTML 1.0 Strict//EN"
    "http://www.w3.org/TR/xhtml1/DTD/xhtml1-strict.dtd">
<html xmlns="http://www.w3.org/1999/xhtml" xml:lang="en" lang="en">
<head>
  <title>Creating Tooltips Using the title Attribute</title>
  <meta http-equiv="Content-Type" content="text/html; charset=utf-8" />
</head>
<body>
<p>Hover over the text to see a tooltip: <span title="This is a tooltip">Hover
here</span></p>
</body>
</html>
```

Creating a Photo Gallery with Thumbnails

```
<!DOCTYPE html PUBLIC "-//W3C//DTD XHTML 1.0 Strict//EN"
    "http://www.w3.org/TR/xhtml1/DTD/xhtml1-strict.dtd">
<html xmlns="http://www.w3.org/1999/xhtml" xml:lang="en" lang="en">
<head>
  <title>Creating a Photo Gallery with Thumbnails</title>
  <meta http-equiv="Content-Type" content="text/html; charset=utf-8" />
  <style type="text/css">
    .gallery {
      display: flex;
      flex-wrap: wrap;
    }
    .gallery img {
      margin: 5px;
      width: 200px;
      height: 150px;
      object-fit: cover;
      cursor: pointer;
      transition: transform 0.3s ease;
    }
    .gallery img:hover {
      transform: scale(1.1);
    }
  </style>
</head>
<body>
<div class="gallery">
  <img src="image1.jpg" alt="Image 1" />
```

```
  <img src="image2.jpg" alt="Image 2" />

  <img src="image3.jpg" alt="Image 3" />

  <!-- Add more images as needed -->

</div>

</body>

</html>
```

Using the <figure> and <figcaption> Elements for Image Captions

```
<!DOCTYPE html PUBLIC "-//W3C//DTD XHTML 1.0 Strict//EN"
    "http://www.w3.org/TR/xhtml1/DTD/xhtml1-strict.dtd">
<html xmlns="http://www.w3.org/1999/xhtml" xml:lang="en" lang="en">
<head>
  <title>Using the &lt;figure&gt; and &lt;figcaption&gt; Elements for Image
Captions</title>
  <meta http-equiv="Content-Type" content="text/html; charset=utf-8" />
  <style type="text/css">
    figure {
      margin: 0;
      padding: 0;
      text-align: center;
    }
    figcaption {
      font-style: italic;
    }
  </style>
</head>
<body>
<figure>
```

```
<img src="example.jpg" alt="Example Image" />

<figcaption>This is a caption for the example image.</figcaption>

</figure>

</body>

</html>
```

Creating a Dropdown Navigation Menu with Hover Effects

```
<!DOCTYPE html PUBLIC "-//W3C//DTD XHTML 1.0 Strict//EN"

    "http://www.w3.org/TR/xhtml1/DTD/xhtml1-strict.dtd">

<html xmlns="http://www.w3.org/1999/xhtml" xml:lang="en" lang="en">

<head>

  <title>Creating a Dropdown Navigation Menu with Hover Effects</title>

  <meta http-equiv="Content-Type" content="text/html; charset=utf-8" />

  <style type="text/css">

    .dropdown {

      position: relative;

      display: inline-block;

    }

    .dropdown-content {

      display: none;

      position: absolute;

      background-color: #f9f9f9;

      min-width: 160px;

      box-shadow: 0px 8px 16px 0px rgba(0,0,0,0.2);

      z-index: 1;

    }

    .dropdown:hover .dropdown-content {

      display: block;
```

```
      }
      .dropdown-content a {
        color: black;
        padding: 12px 16px;
        text-decoration: none;
        display: block;
      }
      .dropdown-content a:hover {background-color: #f1f1f1}
    </style>
</head>
<body>
<div class="dropdown">
  <span>Hover over me</span>
  <div class="dropdown-content">
    <a href="#">Link 1</a>
    <a href="#">Link 2</a>
    <a href="#">Link 3</a>
  </div>
</div>
</body>
</html>
```

Using the <meter> Element for Displaying a Gauge

```
<!DOCTYPE html PUBLIC "-//W3C//DTD XHTML 1.0 Strict//EN"
      "http://www.w3.org/TR/xhtml1/DTD/xhtml1-strict.dtd">
<html xmlns="http://www.w3.org/1999/xhtml" xml:lang="en" lang="en">
<head>
  <title>Using the &lt;meter&gt; Element for Displaying a Gauge</title>
```

```
    <meta http-equiv="Content-Type" content="text/html; charset=utf-8" />
</head>
<body>
<p>Progress: <meter value="6" min="0" max="10">6 out of 10</meter></p>
</body>
</html>
```

Using the <progress> Element for Showing Progress Bars

```
<!DOCTYPE html PUBLIC "-//W3C//DTD XHTML 1.0 Strict//EN"
    "http://www.w3.org/TR/xhtml1/DTD/xhtml1-strict.dtd">
<html xmlns="http://www.w3.org/1999/xhtml" xml:lang="en" lang="en">
<head>
  <title>Using the &lt;progress&gt; Element for Showing Progress Bars</title>
  <meta http-equiv="Content-Type" content="text/html; charset=utf-8" />
</head>
<body>
<p>Downloading progress: <progress value="70"
max="100">70%</progress></p>
</body>
</html>
```

Creating a Responsive Image Grid

```
<!DOCTYPE html PUBLIC "-//W3C//DTD XHTML 1.0 Strict//EN"
    "http://www.w3.org/TR/xhtml1/DTD/xhtml1-strict.dtd">
<html xmlns="http://www.w3.org/1999/xhtml" xml:lang="en" lang="en">
<head>
  <title>Creating a Responsive Image Grid</title>
  <meta http-equiv="Content-Type" content="text/html; charset=utf-8" />
```

```
  <style type="text/css">
    .image-grid {
      display: grid;
      grid-template-columns: repeat(auto-fill, minmax(200px, 1fr));
      grid-gap: 10px;
    }
    .image-grid img {
      width: 100%;
      height: auto;
      display: block;
    }
  </style>
</head>
<body>
<div class="image-grid">
  <img src="image1.jpg" alt="Image 1" />
  <img src="image2.jpg" alt="Image 2" />
  <img src="image3.jpg" alt="Image 3" />
  <!-- Add more images as needed -->
</div>
</body>
</html>
```

Using the <details> and <summary> Elements for Collapsible Content

```
<!DOCTYPE html PUBLIC "-//W3C//DTD XHTML 1.0 Strict//EN"
      "http://www.w3.org/TR/xhtml1/DTD/xhtml1-strict.dtd">
<html xmlns="http://www.w3.org/1999/xhtml" xml:lang="en" lang="en">
<head>
```

```
    <title>Using the &lt;details&gt; and &lt;summary&gt; Elements for
Collapsible Content</title>
    <meta http-equiv="Content-Type" content="text/html; charset=utf-8" />
    <style type="text/css">
      summary {
        cursor: pointer;
        font-weight: bold;
      }
      details > p {
        margin-top: 0;
      }
    </style>
</head>
<body>
<details>
  <summary>Click to expand</summary>
  <p>Hidden content revealed!</p>
</details>
</body>
</html>
```

Creating a Timeline Using Lists and CSS

```
<!DOCTYPE html PUBLIC "-//W3C//DTD XHTML 1.0 Strict//EN"
    "http://www.w3.org/TR/xhtml1/DTD/xhtml1-strict.dtd">
<html xmlns="http://www.w3.org/1999/xhtml" xml:lang="en" lang="en">
<head>
    <title>Creating a Timeline Using Lists and CSS</title>
    <meta http-equiv="Content-Type" content="text/html; charset=utf-8" />
```

```
<style type="text/css">
  .timeline {
    list-style: none;
    padding: 0;
  }
  .timeline li {
    position: relative;
    padding-left: 20px;
    margin-bottom: 20px;
  }
  .timeline li::before {
    content: ";
    position: absolute;
    left: 0;
    top: 5px;
    width: 10px;
    height: 10px;
    background-color: #000;
    border-radius: 50%;
  }
</style>
</head>
<body>
<ul class="timeline">
  <li>Event 1</li>
  <li>Event 2</li>
  <li>Event 3</li>
  <!-- Add more events as needed -->
```

```
</ul>

</body>

</html>
```

Implementing CSS Transitions for Hover Effects

```html
<!DOCTYPE html PUBLIC "-//W3C//DTD XHTML 1.0 Strict//EN"
      "http://www.w3.org/TR/xhtml1/DTD/xhtml1-strict.dtd">
<html xmlns="http://www.w3.org/1999/xhtml" xml:lang="en" lang="en">
<head>
   <title>Implementing CSS Transitions for Hover Effects</title>
   <meta http-equiv="Content-Type" content="text/html; charset=utf-8" />
   <style type="text/css">
     .hover-effect {
        transition: transform 0.3s ease;
     }
     .hover-effect:hover {
        transform: scale(1.1);
     }
   </style>
</head>
<body>
<img src="hover-image.jpg" alt="Hover Image" class="hover-effect" />
</body>
</html>
```

Using the <canvas> Element for Drawing Graphics

```html
<!DOCTYPE html PUBLIC "-//W3C//DTD XHTML 1.0 Strict//EN"
      "http://www.w3.org/TR/xhtml1/DTD/xhtml1-strict.dtd">
```

```
<html xmlns="http://www.w3.org/1999/xhtml" xml:lang="en" lang="en">
<head>
   <title>Using the &lt;canvas&gt; Element for Drawing Graphics</title>
   <meta http-equiv="Content-Type" content="text/html; charset=utf-8" />
   <style type="text/css">
     canvas {
       border: 1px solid #000;
     }
   </style>
</head>
<body>
<canvas id="myCanvas" width="200" height="100">
   Your browser does not support the HTML5 canvas tag.
</canvas>
<script type="text/javascript">
   var canvas = document.getElementById('myCanvas');
   var ctx = canvas.getContext('2d');
   // Draw a red rectangle
   ctx.fillStyle = 'red';
   ctx.fillRect(10, 10, 50, 50);
   // Draw a blue circle
   ctx.beginPath();
   ctx.arc(100, 50, 20, 0, 2 * Math.PI);
   ctx.fillStyle = 'blue';
   ctx.fill();
</script>
</body>
</html>
```

Creating a Basic SVG Graphic and Embedding it in XHTML

```
<!DOCTYPE html PUBLIC "-//W3C//DTD XHTML 1.0 Strict//EN"
     "http://www.w3.org/TR/xhtml1/DTD/xhtml1-strict.dtd">
<html xmlns="http://www.w3.org/1999/xhtml" xml:lang="en" lang="en">
<head>
   <title>Creating a Basic SVG Graphic and Embedding it in XHTML</title>
   <meta http-equiv="Content-Type" content="text/html; charset=utf-8" />
</head>
<body>
<svg width="100" height="100">
   <circle cx="50" cy="50" r="40" stroke="black" stroke-width="2" fill="red" />
</svg>
</body>
</html>
```

Implementing a Simple JavaScript Slideshow with XHTML

```
<!DOCTYPE html PUBLIC "-//W3C//DTD XHTML 1.0 Strict//EN"
     "http://www.w3.org/TR/xhtml1/DTD/xhtml1-strict.dtd">
<html xmlns="http://www.w3.org/1999/xhtml" xml:lang="en" lang="en">
<head>
   <title>Implementing a Simple JavaScript Slideshow with XHTML</title>
   <meta http-equiv="Content-Type" content="text/html; charset=utf-8" />
   <style type="text/css">
     .slideshow {
       position: relative;
       max-width: 100%;
       height: auto;
```

```
      }
      .slideshow img {
         display: block;
         width: 100%;
         height: auto;
      }
   </style>
</head>
<body>
<div class="slideshow">
   <img src="slide1.jpg" alt="Slide 1" />
   <img src="slide2.jpg" alt="Slide 2" />
   <img src="slide3.jpg" alt="Slide 3" />
   <!-- Add more slides as needed -->
</div>
<script type="text/javascript">
   var slides = document.querySelectorAll('.slideshow img');
   var currentSlide = 0;
   function nextSlide() {
      slides[currentSlide].style.display = 'none';
      currentSlide = (currentSlide + 1) % slides.length;
      slides[currentSlide].style.display = 'block';
   }
   setInterval(nextSlide, 3000); // Change slide every 3 seconds
</script>
</body>
</html>
```

Creating a Popup Modal with CSS and XHTML

```
<!DOCTYPE html PUBLIC "-//W3C//DTD XHTML 1.0 Strict//EN"
    "http://www.w3.org/TR/xhtml1/DTD/xhtml1-strict.dtd">
<html xmlns="http://www.w3.org/1999/xhtml" xml:lang="en" lang="en">
<head>
  <title>Creating a Popup Modal with CSS and XHTML</title>
  <meta http-equiv="Content-Type" content="text/html; charset=utf-8" />
  <style type="text/css">
    .modal {
      display: none;
      position: fixed;
      z-index: 1;
      left: 0;
      top: 0;
      width: 100%;
      height: 100%;
      overflow: auto;
      background-color: rgba(0,0,0,0.5);
    }
    .modal-content {
      background-color: #fefefe;
      margin: 15% auto;
      padding: 20px;
      border: 1px solid #888;
      width: 80%;
    }
    .close {
```

```
      color: #aaa;

      float: right;

      font-size: 28px;

      font-weight: bold;

    }

    .close:hover,

    .close:focus {

      color: black;

      text-decoration: none;

      cursor: pointer;

    }

  </style>

</head>

<body>

<!-- Button to open the modal -->

<button onclick="openModal()">Open Modal</button>

<!-- The Modal -->

<div id="myModal" class="modal">

  <!-- Modal content -->

  <div class="modal-content">

    <span class="close" onclick="closeModal()">&times;</span>

    <p>This is a modal popup.</p>

  </div>

</div>

<script type="text/javascript">

  // Get the modal

  var modal = document.getElementById('myModal');
```

```
    // Function to open the modal
    function openModal() {
        modal.style.display = 'block';
    }
    // Function to close the modal
    function closeModal() {
        modal.style.display = 'none';
    }
    // Close the modal if user clicks outside of it
    window.onclick = function(event) {
        if (event.target == modal) {
            modal.style.display = 'none';
        }
    }
</script>
</body>
</html>
```

Implementing a Tabbed Navigation Interface

```
<!DOCTYPE html PUBLIC "-//W3C//DTD XHTML 1.0 Strict//EN"
    "http://www.w3.org/TR/xhtml1/DTD/xhtml1-strict.dtd">
<html xmlns="http://www.w3.org/1999/xhtml" xml:lang="en" lang="en">
<head>
    <title>Implementing a Tabbed Navigation Interface</title>
    <meta http-equiv="Content-Type" content="text/html; charset=utf-8" />
    <style type="text/css">
        .tab {
            display: none;
```

```
      }
    .tab.active {
      display: block;
    }
  </style>
</head>
<body>
<div class="tabs">
  <button onclick="openTab(event, 'tab1')">Tab 1</button>
  <button onclick="openTab(event, 'tab2')">Tab 2</button>
  <button onclick="openTab(event, 'tab3')">Tab 3</button>
</div>
<div id="tab1" class="tab active">
  <h2>Tab 1 Content</h2>
  <p>This is the content of tab 1.</p>
</div>
<div id="tab2" class="tab">
  <h2>Tab 2 Content</h2>
  <p>This is the content of tab 2.</p>
</div>
<div id="tab3" class="tab">
  <h2>Tab 3 Content</h2>
  <p>This is the content of tab 3.</p>
</div>
<script type="text/javascript">
  function openTab(event, tabId) {
    var i, tabs, tabLinks;
    tabs = document.getElementsByClassName('tab');
```

```
    for (i = 0; i < tabs.length; i++) {

      tabs[i].classList.remove('active');

    }

    document.getElementById(tabId).classList.add('active');

  }
```

</script>

</body>

</html>

Creating a Sticky/Fixed Header

```
<!DOCTYPE html PUBLIC "-//W3C//DTD XHTML 1.0 Strict//EN"
    "http://www.w3.org/TR/xhtml1/DTD/xhtml1-strict.dtd">
<html xmlns="http://www.w3.org/1999/xhtml" xml:lang="en" lang="en">
<head>
  <title>Creating a Sticky/Fixed Header</title>
  <meta http-equiv="Content-Type" content="text/html; charset=utf-8" />
  <style type="text/css">
    body {
      font-family: Arial, sans-serif;
      margin: 0;
    }
    .header {
      background-color: #333;
      color: #fff;
      text-align: center;
      padding: 10px 0;
      position: fixed;
      width: 100%;
```

```
      top: 0;

      left: 0;

      z-index: 1000;

    }

    .content {

      padding-top: 60px; /* Adjust this value to match the header height */

      height: 1500px; /* Just for demonstration */

    }

  </style>

</head>

<body>

<div class="header">

  <h1>Sticky Header</h1>

</div>

<div class="content">

  <p>This is the main content area.</p>

  <p>*** </p>

</div>

</body>

</html>
```

Implementing a Simple Lightbox Effect for Images

```
<!DOCTYPE html PUBLIC "-//W3C//DTD XHTML 1.0 Strict//EN"

    "http://www.w3.org/TR/xhtml1/DTD/xhtml1-strict.dtd">

<html xmlns="http://www.w3.org/1999/xhtml" xml:lang="en" lang="en">

<head>

  <title>Implementing a Simple Lightbox Effect for Images</title>

  <meta http-equiv="Content-Type" content="text/html; charset=utf-8" />
```

```
<style type="text/css">
    .lightbox {
        display: none;
        position: fixed;
        z-index: 1000;
        left: 0;
        top: 0;
        width: 100%;
        height: 100%;
        background-color: rgba(0,0,0,0.7);
        text-align: center;
    }
    .lightbox img {
        max-width: 80%;
        max-height: 80%;
        margin-top: 10%;
        border: 5px solid #fff;
        box-shadow: 0 0 15px #000;
    }
    .close {
        color: #fff;
        font-size: 30px;
        position: absolute;
        top: 20px;
        right: 30px;
        cursor: pointer;
    }
</style>
```

```
</head>
<body>
<img src="image1.jpg" alt="Image 1" onclick="openLightbox(this)" />
<div id="myModal" class="lightbox">
   <span class="close" onclick="closeLightbox()">&times;</span>
   <img src="image1.jpg" alt="Image 1" />
</div>
<script type="text/javascript">
   function openLightbox(image) {
      var modal = document.getElementById('myModal');
      var modalImg = modal.querySelector('img');
      modal.style.display = 'block';
      modalImg.src = image.src;
   }
   function closeLightbox() {
      document.getElementById('myModal').style.display = 'none';
   }
</script>
</body>
</html>
```

Creating a Multi-column Layout Using CSS and XHTML

```
<!DOCTYPE html PUBLIC "-//W3C//DTD XHTML 1.0 Strict//EN"
      "http://www.w3.org/TR/xhtml1/DTD/xhtml1-strict.dtd">
<html xmlns="http://www.w3.org/1999/xhtml" xml:lang="en" lang="en">
<head>
   <title>Creating a Multi-column Layout Using CSS and XHTML</title>
   <meta http-equiv="Content-Type" content="text/html; charset=utf-8" />
```

```
    <style type="text/css">
      .container {
        display: grid;
        grid-template-columns: repeat(3, 1fr);
        grid-gap: 20px;
        padding: 20px;
      }
      .box {
        background-color: #f0f0f0;
        padding: 15px;
        border: 1px solid #ccc;
        text-align: center;
      }
    </style>
  </head>
  <body>
  <div class="container">
    <div class="box">Column 1</div>
    <div class="box">Column 2</div>
    <div class="box">Column 3</div>
    <div class="box">Column 4</div>
    <div class="box">Column 5</div>
    <div class="box">Column 6</div>
  </div>
  </body>
</html>
```

Implementing Smooth Scrolling to Anchor Links

```
<!DOCTYPE html PUBLIC "-//W3C//DTD XHTML 1.0 Strict//EN"
    "http://www.w3.org/TR/xhtml1/DTD/xhtml1-strict.dtd">
<html xmlns="http://www.w3.org/1999/xhtml" xml:lang="en" lang="en">
<head>
  <title>Implementing Smooth Scrolling to Anchor Links</title>
  <meta http-equiv="Content-Type" content="text/html; charset=utf-8" />
  <style type="text/css">
    .menu {
      position: fixed;
      top: 0;
      left: 0;
      width: 100%;
      background-color: #333;
      color: #fff;
      text-align: center;
      padding: 10px 0;
      z-index: 1000;
    }
    .content {
      padding-top: 60px; /* Adjust this value to match the menu height */
      height: 2000px; /* Just for demonstration */
    }
    .section {
      padding: 20px;
      margin: 20px 0;
      background-color: #f0f0f0;
    }
```

```
    </style>
</head>
<body>
<div class="menu">
  <a href="#section1">Section 1</a> |
  <a href="#section2">Section 2</a> |
  <a href="#section3">Section 3</a>
</div>
<div class="content">
  <div id="section1" class="section">
    <h2>Section 1</h2>
    <p>This is section 1 content.</p>
  </div>
  <div id="section2" class="section">
    <h2>Section 2</h2>
    <p>This is section 2 content.</p>
  </div>
  <div id="section3" class="section">
    <h2>Section 3</h2>
    <p>This is section 3 content.</p>
  </div>
</div>
<script type="text/javascript">
  document.querySelectorAll('a[href^="#"]').forEach(anchor => {
    anchor.addEventListener('click', function(e) {
      e.preventDefault();
      document.querySelector(this.getAttribute('href')).scrollIntoView({
        behavior: 'smooth'
```

```
      });
    });
  });
</script>
</body>
</html>
```

Using CSS Grid for Layout

```
<!DOCTYPE html PUBLIC "-//W3C//DTD XHTML 1.0 Strict//EN"
    "http://www.w3.org/TR/xhtml1/DTD/xhtml1-strict.dtd">
<html xmlns="http://www.w3.org/1999/xhtml" xml:lang="en" lang="en">
<head>
  <title>Using CSS Grid for Layout</title>
  <meta http-equiv="Content-Type" content="text/html; charset=utf-8" />
  <style type="text/css">
    .grid-container {
      display: grid;
      grid-template-columns: repeat(3, 1fr);
      grid-gap: 10px;
      padding: 10px;
    }
    .grid-item {
      background-color: #f0f0f0;
      padding: 20px;
      border: 1px solid #ccc;
      text-align: center;
    }
  </style>
```

```
</head>

<body>

<div class="grid-container">

    <div class="grid-item">Item 1</div>

    <div class="grid-item">Item 2</div>

    <div class="grid-item">Item 3</div>

    <div class="grid-item">Item 4</div>

    <div class="grid-item">Item 5</div>

    <div class="grid-item">Item 6</div>

</div>

</body>

</html>
```

Using CSS Flexbox for Layout

```
<!DOCTYPE html PUBLIC "-//W3C//DTD XHTML 1.0 Strict//EN"

    "http://www.w3.org/TR/xhtml1/DTD/xhtml1-strict.dtd">

<html xmlns="http://www.w3.org/1999/xhtml" xml:lang="en" lang="en">

<head>

    <title>Using CSS Flexbox for Layout</title>

    <meta http-equiv="Content-Type" content="text/html; charset=utf-8" />

    <style type="text/css">

        .flex-container {

            display: flex;

            justify-content: space-between;

            align-items: center;

            height: 100px;

            background-color: #333;

            color: #fff;
```

```
      padding: 0 20px;
    }
    .item {
      flex: 1;
    }
  </style>
</head>
<body>
<div class="flex-container">
  <div class="item">Item 1</div>
  <div class="item">Item 2</div>
  <div class="item">Item 3</div>
</div>
</body>
</html>
```

Implementing a Dropdown Mega Menu

```
<!DOCTYPE html PUBLIC "-//W3C//DTD XHTML 1.0 Strict//EN"
    "http://www.w3.org/TR/xhtml1/DTD/xhtml1-strict.dtd">
<html xmlns="http://www.w3.org/1999/xhtml" xml:lang="en" lang="en">
<head>
  <title>Implementing a Dropdown Mega Menu</title>
  <meta http-equiv="Content-Type" content="text/html; charset=utf-8" />
  <style type="text/css">
    .menu {
      list-style-type: none;
      padding: 0;
      background-color: #333;
```

```
    color: #fff;

    display: flex;

    justify-content: space-between;

    align-items: center;

    height: 50px;

  }

  .menu li {

    position: relative;

    cursor: pointer;

    padding: 0 15px;

    line-height: 50px;

  }

  .dropdown {

    display: none;

    position: absolute;

    top: 50px;

    left: 0;

    background-color: #555;

    min-width: 200px;

    z-index: 1000;

  }

  .dropdown li {

    padding: 10px;

  }

  .menu li:hover .dropdown {

    display: block;

  }
```
</style>

```
</head>
<body>
<ul class="menu">
  <li>Home</li>
  <li>About
    <ul class="dropdown">
      <li>History</li>
      <li>Mission</li>
      <li>Vision</li>
    </ul>
  </li>
  <li>Services
    <ul class="dropdown">
      <li>Web Design</li>
      <li>Graphic Design</li>
      <li>SEO</li>
    </ul>
  </li>
  <li>Contact</li>
</ul>
</body>
</html>
```

Creating a Responsive Navigation Menu with a Hamburger Icon

```
<!DOCTYPE html PUBLIC "-//W3C//DTD XHTML 1.0 Strict//EN"
    "http://www.w3.org/TR/xhtml1/DTD/xhtml1-strict.dtd">
<html xmlns="http://www.w3.org/1999/xhtml" xml:lang="en" lang="en">
<head>
```

```
<title>Creating a Responsive Navigation Menu with a Hamburger Icon</title>
<meta http-equiv="Content-Type" content="text/html; charset=utf-8" />
<style type="text/css">
  .nav {
    background-color: #333;
    color: #fff;
    display: flex;
    justify-content: space-between;
    align-items: center;
    padding: 10px 20px;
  }
  .nav .logo {
    font-size: 24px;
    font-weight: bold;
  }
  .nav .menu {
    display: flex;
    list-style-type: none;
    padding: 0;
    margin: 0;
  }
  .nav .menu li {
    padding: 0 10px;
    cursor: pointer;
  }
  .nav .menu li:hover {
    background-color: #555;
  }
```

```
        .nav .menu-icon {
            display: none;
            font-size: 24px;
            cursor: pointer;
        }
        @media screen and (max-width: 768px) {
            .nav .menu {
                display: none;
                flex-direction: column;
                position: absolute;
                top: 60px;
                left: 0;
                width: 100%;
                background-color: #333;
                z-index: 1000;
            }
            .nav .menu.show {
                display: flex;
            }
            .nav .menu-icon {
                display: block;
            }
        }
    </style>
</head>
<body>
<nav class="nav">
  <div class="logo">Logo</div>
```

```
    <div class="menu-icon" onclick="toggleMenu()">&#9776;</div>

    <ul class="menu">

      <li>Home</li>

      <li>About</li>

      <li>Services</li>

      <li>Contact</li>

    </ul>

</nav>

<script type="text/javascript">

  function toggleMenu() {

    var menu = document.querySelector('.menu');

    menu.classList.toggle('show');

  }

</script>

</body>

</html>
```

Using CSS Animations for Interactive Elements

```
<!DOCTYPE html PUBLIC "-//W3C//DTD XHTML 1.0 Strict//EN"

    "http://www.w3.org/TR/xhtml11/DTD/xhtml11-strict.dtd">

<html xmlns="http://www.w3.org/1999/xhtml" xml:lang="en" lang="en">

<head>

  <title>Using CSS Animations for Interactive Elements</title>

  <meta http-equiv="Content-Type" content="text/html; charset=utf-8" />

  <style type="text/css">

    .btn {

      padding: 10px 20px;

      background-color: #333;
```

```css
      color: #fff;

      font-size: 16px;

      border: none;

      cursor: pointer;

      position: relative;

      overflow: hidden;

      transition: background-color 0.3s;

    }

    .btn::after {

      content: ";

      position: absolute;

      top: 50%;

      left: 50%;

      width: 300px;

      height: 300px;

      background-color: rgba(255, 255, 255, 0.1);

      transition: width 0.4s, height 0.4s, top 0.4s, left 0.4s;

      border-radius: 50%;

      transform: translate(-50%, -50%) scale(0);

    }

    .btn:hover::after {

      width: 0;

      height: 0;

      top: 50%;

      left: 50%;

    }
  </style>
</head>
```

```
<body>

<button class="btn">Hover Me</button>

</body>

</html>
```

Implementing Form Validation using JavaScript and XHTML

```
<!DOCTYPE html PUBLIC "-//W3C//DTD XHTML 1.0 Strict//EN"
    "http://www.w3.org/TR/xhtml11/DTD/xhtml11-strict.dtd">
<html xmlns="http://www.w3.org/1999/xhtml" xml:lang="en" lang="en">
<head>
  <title>Implementing Form Validation using JavaScript and XHTML</title>
  <meta http-equiv="Content-Type" content="text/html; charset=utf-8" />
  <style type="text/css">
    .form {
      max-width: 400px;
      margin: 20px auto;
      padding: 20px;
      border: 1px solid #ccc;
      background-color: #f0f0f0;
    }
    .form input {
      width: 100%;
      padding: 10px;
      margin: 10px 0;
      box-sizing: border-box;
    }
    .form button {
      padding: 10px 20px;
```

```
      background-color: #333;

      color: #fff;

      border: none;

      cursor: pointer;

    }

    .form button:hover {

      background-color: #555;

    }

  </style>

</head>

<body>

<form class="form" onsubmit="return validateForm()">

  <input type="text" id="name" name="name" placeholder="Your Name"
required />

  <br />

  <input type="email" id="email" name="email" placeholder="Your Email"
required />

  <br />

  <button type="submit">Submit</button>

</form>

<script type="text/javascript">

  function validateForm() {

    var name = document.getElementById('name').value;

    var email = document.getElementById('email').value;

    if (name.trim() === '' || email.trim() === '') {

      alert('Please fill out all fields');

      return false;

    }
```

```
      return true;

   }

</script>

</body>

</html>
```

Creating a Countdown Timer using JavaScript and XHTML

```
<!DOCTYPE html PUBLIC "-//W3C//DTD XHTML 1.0 Strict//EN"
      "http://www.w3.org/TR/xhtml1/DTD/xhtml1-strict.dtd">
<html xmlns="http://www.w3.org/1999/xhtml" xml:lang="en" lang="en">
<head>
   <title>Creating a Countdown Timer using JavaScript and XHTML</title>
   <meta http-equiv="Content-Type" content="text/html; charset=utf-8" />
   <style type="text/css">
      .countdown {
         text-align: center;
         font-size: 24px;
         margin-top: 20px;
      }
   </style>
</head>
<body>
<div class="countdown" id="countdown"></div>
<script type="text/javascript">
   // Set the countdown date (e.g., 1 hour from now)
   var countdownDate = new Date();
   countdownDate.setHours(countdownDate.getHours() + 1); // 1 hour from now
   // Update the countdown every second
```

```
    var countdownInterval = setInterval(function() {

      var now = new Date().getTime();

      var distance = countdownDate - now;

      // Calculating remaining time

      var hours = Math.floor((distance % (1000 * 60 * 60 * 24)) / (1000 * 60 *
60));

      var minutes = Math.floor((distance % (1000 * 60 * 60)) / (1000 * 60));

      var seconds = Math.floor((distance % (1000 * 60)) / 1000);

      // Displaying the countdown

      document.getElementById('countdown').innerHTML = hours + "h "

        + minutes + "m " + seconds + "s ";

      // If the countdown is finished, show a message

      if (distance < 0) {

        clearInterval(countdownInterval);

        document.getElementById('countdown').innerHTML = "EXPIRED";

      }

    }, 1000); // Update every second
</script>
</body>
</html>
```

Implementing a Character Counter for Textarea Inputs

```
<!DOCTYPE html PUBLIC "-//W3C//DTD XHTML 1.0 Strict//EN"
        "http://www.w3.org/TR/xhtml1/DTD/xhtml1-strict.dtd">
<html xmlns="http://www.w3.org/1999/xhtml" xml:lang="en" lang="en">
<head>
  <title>Implementing a Character Counter for Textarea Inputs</title>
  <meta http-equiv="Content-Type" content="text/html; charset=utf-8" />
```

```
  <style type="text/css">
    .textarea-container {
      margin: 20px;
    }
    .counter {
      color: #999;
      font-size: 12px;
    }
  </style>
</head>
<body>
<div class="textarea-container">
  <textarea id="message" rows="4" cols="50" maxlength="200"
oninput="updateCounter()"></textarea>
  <div class="counter" id="counter">Characters remaining: 200</div>
</div>
<script type="text/javascript">
  function updateCounter() {
    var maxLength = 200;
    var currentLength = document.getElementById('message').value.length;
    var remaining = maxLength - currentLength;
    document.getElementById('counter').innerHTML = 'Characters remaining: '
+ remaining;
  }
</script>
</body>
</html>
```

Creating a Responsive Carousel/Slider

```
<!DOCTYPE html PUBLIC "-//W3C//DTD XHTML 1.0 Strict//EN"
    "http://www.w3.org/TR/xhtml1/DTD/xhtml1-strict.dtd">
<html xmlns="http://www.w3.org/1999/xhtml" xml:lang="en" lang="en">
<head>
  <title>Creating a Responsive Carousel/Slider</title>
  <meta http-equiv="Content-Type" content="text/html; charset=utf-8" />
  <style type="text/css">
    .carousel {
      display: flex;
      overflow-x: auto;
      scroll-snap-type: x mandatory;
      -webkit-overflow-scrolling: touch; /* Enables smooth scrolling on iOS */
      width: 100%;
      height: 300px;
    }
    .carousel-item {
      flex: 0 0 auto;
      scroll-snap-align: start;
      width: 100%;
      height: 100%;
      background-color: #f0f0f0;
      text-align: center;
      font-size: 24px;
      display: flex;
      justify-content: center;
      align-items: center;
    }
```

```
  </style>
</head>
<body>
<div class="carousel">
   <div class="carousel-item">Slide 1</div>
   <div class="carousel-item">Slide 2</div>
   <div class="carousel-item">Slide 3</div>
   <div class="carousel-item">Slide 4</div>
   <div class="carousel-item">Slide 5</div>
</div>
</body>
</html>
```

Using XHTML Data Attributes for Storing Extra Information

```
<!DOCTYPE html PUBLIC "-//W3C//DTD XHTML 1.0 Strict//EN"
      "http://www.w3.org/TR/xhtml1/DTD/xhtml1-strict.dtd">
<html xmlns="http://www.w3.org/1999/xhtml" xml:lang="en" lang="en">
<head>
   <title>Using XHTML Data Attributes for Storing Extra Information</title>
   <meta http-equiv="Content-Type" content="text/html; charset=utf-8" />
   <style type="text/css">
      .product {
         border: 1px solid #ccc;
         padding: 10px;
         margin: 10px;
      }
      .product h2 {
         font-size: 18px;
```

```
      margin-bottom: 5px;
    }
    .product p {
      margin: 0;
    }
  </style>
</head>
<body>
<div class="product" data-id="1" data-price="50">
  <h2>Product A</h2>
  <p>Description of Product A.</p>
  <p>Price: $50</p>
</div>
<div class="product" data-id="2" data-price="70">
  <h2>Product B</h2>
  <p>Description of Product B.</p>
  <p>Price: $70</p>
</div>
<script type="text/javascript">
  // Example JavaScript to retrieve data attributes
  var products = document.querySelectorAll('.product');
  products.forEach(function(product) {
    var productId = product.getAttribute('data-id');
    var productPrice = product.getAttribute('data-price');
    console.log('Product ID:', productId);
    console.log('Product Price:', productPrice);
  });
</script>
```

```
</body>

</html>
```

Implementing a "Load More" Button for Dynamic Content

```
<!DOCTYPE html PUBLIC "-//W3C//DTD XHTML 1.0 Strict//EN"
    "http://www.w3.org/TR/xhtml1/DTD/xhtml1-strict.dtd">
<html xmlns="http://www.w3.org/1999/xhtml" xml:lang="en" lang="en">
<head>
  <title>Implementing a "Load More" Button for Dynamic Content</title>
  <meta http-equiv="Content-Type" content="text/html; charset=utf-8" />
  <style type="text/css">
    .content {
      margin: 20px;
    }
    .item {
      padding: 10px;
      border: 1px solid #ccc;
      margin-bottom: 10px;
    }
    .load-more-btn {
      display: block;
      margin: 20px auto;
      padding: 10px 20px;
      background-color: #333;
      color: #fff;
      border: none;
      cursor: pointer;
    }
```

```
    .load-more-btn:hover {
        background-color: #555;
    }
    .hidden {
        display: none;
    }
  </style>
</head>
<body>
<div class="content" id="content">
  <div class="item">Item 1</div>
  <div class="item">Item 2</div>
  <div class="item">Item 3</div>
  <div class="item hidden">Item 4</div>
  <div class="item hidden">Item 5</div>
  <div class="item hidden">Item 6</div>
</div>
<button class="load-more-btn" onclick="loadMore()">Load More</button>
<script type="text/javascript">
    function loadMore() {
        var hiddenItems = document.querySelectorAll('.hidden');
        hiddenItems.forEach(function(item, index) {
            if (index < 3) { // Load 3 more items at a time
                item.classList.remove('hidden');
            }
        });
        // Hide the load more button if no more hidden items
        var allItems = document.querySelectorAll('.item');
```

```
    if (hiddenItems.length === 0) {

      document.querySelector('.load-more-btn').style.display = 'none';

    }

  }

</script>

</body>

</html>
```

Creating a Sticky Footer that Stays at the Bottom of the Page

```
<!DOCTYPE html PUBLIC "-//W3C//DTD XHTML 1.0 Strict//EN"

    "http://www.w3.org/TR/xhtml11/DTD/xhtml11-strict.dtd">

<html xmlns="http://www.w3.org/1999/xhtml" xml:lang="en" lang="en">

<head>

  <title>Creating a Sticky Footer that Stays at the Bottom of the Page</title>

  <meta http-equiv="Content-Type" content="text/html; charset=utf-8" />

  <style type="text/css">

    html, body {

      height: 100%;

      margin: 0;

    }

    .wrapper {

      min-height: 100%;

      margin-bottom: -100px;

      padding-bottom: 100px;

    }

    .footer {

      height: 100px;

      background-color: #333;
```

```
        color: #fff;
        text-align: center;
        line-height: 100px;
      }
    </style>
  </head>
  <body>
  <div class="wrapper">
    <div class="content">
      <!-- Your content goes here -->
    </div>
  </div>
  <div class="footer">
    Sticky Footer
  </div>
  </body>
  </html>
```

Implementing Parallax Scrolling Effects

```
<!DOCTYPE html PUBLIC "-//W3C//DTD XHTML 1.0 Strict//EN"
      "http://www.w3.org/TR/xhtml1/DTD/xhtml1-strict.dtd">
<html xmlns="http://www.w3.org/1999/xhtml" xml:lang="en" lang="en">
<head>
    <title>Implementing Parallax Scrolling Effects</title>
    <meta http-equiv="Content-Type" content="text/html; charset=utf-8" />
    <style type="text/css">
      .parallax-container {
        height: 400px;
```

```
      background-image: url('background.jpg');

      background-size: cover;

      background-attachment: fixed;

      background-position: center;

      overflow-x: hidden;

      position: relative;

    }

    .parallax-content {

      position: absolute;

      top: 50%;

      left: 50%;

      transform: translate(-50%, -50%);

      text-align: center;

      color: #fff;

      font-size: 36px;

    }

  </style>

</head>

<body>

<div class="parallax-container">

  <div class="parallax-content">

    Parallax Scrolling Effect

  </div>

</div>

<div style="height: 1000px;">

  <!-- Some content to scroll -->

</div>

</body> </html>
```

Creating a 404 Error Page with a Custom Design

```
<!DOCTYPE html PUBLIC "-//W3C//DTD XHTML 1.0 Strict//EN"
    "http://www.w3.org/TR/xhtml1/DTD/xhtml1-strict.dtd">
<html xmlns="http://www.w3.org/1999/xhtml" xml:lang="en" lang="en">
<head>
  <title>404 Error - Page Not Found</title>
  <meta http-equiv="Content-Type" content="text/html; charset=utf-8" />
  <style type="text/css">
    body {
      background-color: #f0f0f0;
      font-family: Arial, sans-serif;
      display: flex;
      justify-content: center;
      align-items: center;
      height: 100vh;
      margin: 0;
    }
    .error-container {
      text-align: center;
    }
    .error-code {
      font-size: 72px;
      color: #333;
      margin-bottom: 10px;
    }
    .error-message {
      font-size: 24px;
      color: #555;
```

```
      margin-bottom: 20px;
    }
    .back-link {
      text-decoration: none;
      color: #777;
      padding: 10px 20px;
      background-color: #eee;
      border-radius: 5px;
    }
    .back-link:hover {
      background-color: #ddd;
    }
  </style>
</head>
<body>
<div class="error-container">
  <div class="error-code">404</div>
  <div class="error-message">Oops! Page not found.</div>
  <a href="/" class="back-link">Go Back to Homepage</a>
</div>
</body>
</html>
```

Implementing Lazy Loading for Images

```
<!DOCTYPE html PUBLIC "-//W3C//DTD XHTML 1.0 Strict//EN"
    "http://www.w3.org/TR/xhtml1/DTD/xhtml1-strict.dtd">
<html xmlns="http://www.w3.org/1999/xhtml" xml:lang="en" lang="en">
<head>
```

```
  <title>Implementing Lazy Loading for Images</title>
  <meta http-equiv="Content-Type" content="text/html; charset=utf-8" />
  <style type="text/css">
    .image-container {
      width: 100%;
      height: 400px;
      background-color: #f0f0f0;
      position: relative;
    }
    .lazy-img {
      position: absolute;
      top: 0;
      left: 0;
      width: 100%;
      height: 100%;
      transition: opacity 0.3s ease;
    }
    .lazy-img.loading {
      opacity: 0;
    }
  </style>
</head>
<body>
<div class="image-container">
  <img data-src="image.jpg" class="lazy-img" alt="Lazy Loaded Image" />
</div>
<script type="text/javascript">
  document.addEventListener('DOMContentLoaded', function() {
```

```
      var lazyImages = document.querySelectorAll('.lazy-img');
      function lazyLoad() {
        lazyImages.forEach(function(img) {
          if (img.getBoundingClientRect().top < window.innerHeight &&
!img.src) {
                img.src = img.getAttribute('data-src');
                img.onload = function() {
                  img.classList.remove('loading');
                };
            }
          });
      }
      window.addEventListener('scroll', lazyLoad);
      lazyLoad(); // Initial load
    });
</script>
</body>
</html>
```

Using XHTML for Accessibility Enhancements (ARIA Attributes)

```
<!DOCTYPE html PUBLIC "-//W3C//DTD XHTML 1.0 Strict//EN"
    "http://www.w3.org/TR/xhtml1/DTD/xhtml1-strict.dtd">
<html xmlns="http://www.w3.org/1999/xhtml" xml:lang="en" lang="en">
<head>
  <title>Using XHTML for Accessibility Enhancements (ARIA
Attributes)</title>
  <meta http-equiv="Content-Type" content="text/html; charset=utf-8" />
</head>
```

```
<body>
<h1>Accessible Form Example</h1>
<form action="#" method="post">
   <label for="name">Name:</label>
   <input type="text" id="name" name="name" aria-label="Enter your name"
aria-required="true" required />
   <label for="email">Email:</label>
   <input type="email" id="email" name="email" aria-label="Enter your email"
aria-required="true" required />
   <button type="submit">Submit</button>
</form>
</body>
</html>
```

Implementing a Back-to-Top Button with Smooth Scrolling

```
<!DOCTYPE html PUBLIC "-//W3C//DTD XHTML 1.0 Strict//EN"
     "http://www.w3.org/TR/xhtml1/DTD/xhtml1-strict.dtd">
<html xmlns="http://www.w3.org/1999/xhtml" xml:lang="en" lang="en">
<head>
   <title>Implementing a Back-to-Top Button with Smooth Scrolling</title>
   <meta http-equiv="Content-Type" content="text/html; charset=utf-8" />
   <style type="text/css">
     .back-to-top {
        display: none;
        position: fixed;
        bottom: 20px;
        right: 20px;
        background-color: #333;
```

```
        color: #fff;

        width: 40px;

        height: 40px;

        text-align: center;

        line-height: 40px;

        font-size: 20px;

        border-radius: 50%;

        cursor: pointer;

        transition: opacity 0.3s ease;

      }

      .back-to-top:hover {

        background-color: #555;

      }

    </style>

</head>

<body>

<div style="height: 2000px;">

    <!-- Content to make scrolling possible -->

</div>

<button onclick="backToTop()" class="back-to-top" id="backToTopBtn"

title="Back to Top">↑</button>

<script type="text/javascript">

    window.addEventListener('scroll', function() {

        var backToTopButton = document.getElementById('backToTopBtn');

        if (document.body.scrollTop > 20 || document.documentElement.scrollTop

> 20) {

            backToTopButton.style.display = 'block';

        } else {
```

```
      backToTopButton.style.display = 'none';
    }
  });
  function backToTop() {
    window.scrollTo({top: 0, behavior: 'smooth'});
  }
</script>
</body>
</html>
```

Creating a Newsletter Signup Form with Validation

```
<!DOCTYPE html PUBLIC "-//W3C//DTD XHTML 1.0 Strict//EN"
     "http://www.w3.org/TR/xhtml1/DTD/xhtml1-strict.dtd">
<html xmlns="http://www.w3.org/1999/xhtml" xml:lang="en" lang="en">
<head>
  <title>Creating a Newsletter Signup Form with Validation</title>
  <meta http-equiv="Content-Type" content="text/html; charset=utf-8" />
  <style type="text/css">
    .form-container {
       width: 300px;
       margin: 20px auto;
       padding: 20px;
       border: 1px solid #ccc;
       background-color: #f0f0f0;
    }
    .form-group {
       margin-bottom: 10px;
    }
```

```
    .form-group label {
        display: block;
        margin-bottom: 5px;
    }
    .form-group input {
        width: 100%;
        padding: 5px;
        font-size: 14px;
    }
    .form-group .error-message {
        color: red;
        font-size: 12px;
    }
    .submit-btn {
        display: block;
        width: 100%;
        padding: 10px;
        background-color: #333;
        color: #fff;
        border: none;
        cursor: pointer;
    }
    .submit-btn:hover {
        background-color: #555;
    }
  </style>
</head>
<body>
```

```
<div class="form-container">
   <form action="#" method="post" onsubmit="return validateForm()">
      <div class="form-group">
         <label for="email">Email:</label>
         <input type="email" id="email" name="email" required />
         <div class="error-message" id="emailError"></div>
      </div>
      <button type="submit" class="submit-btn">Subscribe</button>
   </form>
</div>
<script type="text/javascript">
   function validateForm() {
      var emailInput = document.getElementById('email');
      var emailError = document.getElementById('emailError');
      if (!emailInput.checkValidity()) {
         emailError.innerHTML = 'Please enter a valid email address.';
         return false;
      }
      // Perform additional validation if needed
      return true;
   }
</script>
</body>
</html>
```

Implementing a Search Bar with Autocomplete Suggestions

```
<!DOCTYPE html PUBLIC "-//W3C//DTD XHTML 1.0 Strict//EN"
    "http://www.w3.org/TR/xhtml1/DTD/xhtml1-strict.dtd">
```

```
<html xmlns="http://www.w3.org/1999/xhtml" xml:lang="en" lang="en">

<head>

    <title>Implementing a Search Bar with Autocomplete Suggestions</title>

    <meta http-equiv="Content-Type" content="text/html; charset=utf-8" />

    <style type="text/css">

      .search-container {

        width: 300px;

        margin: 20px auto;

      }

      .search-input {

        width: 100%;

        padding: 10px;

        font-size: 14px;

      }

      .suggestions {

        margin-top: 5px;

        background-color: #f0f0f0;

        border: 1px solid #ccc;

        display: none;

        max-height: 200px;

        overflow-y: auto;

      }

      .suggestion-item {

        padding: 10px;

        cursor: pointer;

      }

      .suggestion-item:hover {

        background-color: #e0e0e0;
```

```
        }
    </style>
</head>
<body>
<div class="search-container">
    <input type="text" id="searchInput" class="search-input"
placeholder="Search..." autocomplete="off" />
    <div class="suggestions" id="suggestions"></div>
</div>
<script type="text/javascript">
    var searchInput = document.getElementById('searchInput');
    var suggestions = document.getElementById('suggestions');
    searchInput.addEventListener('input', function() {
        var query = this.value.trim().toLowerCase();
        suggestions.innerHTML = '';
        if (query.length === 0) {
            suggestions.style.display = 'none';
            return;
        }
        // Example suggestions (replace with your own implementation)
        var data = ['apple', 'banana', 'cherry', 'date', 'elderberry', 'fig'];
        var filtered = data.filter(function(item) {
            return item.toLowerCase().indexOf(query) !== -1;
        });
        filtered.forEach(function(item) {
            var suggestion = document.createElement('div');
            suggestion.classList.add('suggestion-item');
            suggestion.textContent = item;
```

```
        suggestion.addEventListener('click', function() {

            searchInput.value = item;

            suggestions.style.display = 'none';

        });

        suggestions.appendChild(suggestion);

    });

    suggestions.style.display = filtered.length > 0 ? 'block' : 'none';

});

document.addEventListener('click', function(e) {

    if (!suggestions.contains(e.target)) {

        suggestions.style.display = 'none';

    }

});
</script>
</body>
</html>
```

Using XHTML for Internationalization (Language Attributes)

```
<!DOCTYPE html PUBLIC "-//W3C//DTD XHTML 1.0 Strict//EN"
    "http://www.w3.org/TR/xhtml11/DTD/xhtml11-strict.dtd">
<html xmlns="http://www.w3.org/1999/xhtml" xml:lang="en" lang="en">
<head>
    <title>Using XHTML for Internationalization (Language Attributes)</title>
    <meta http-equiv="Content-Type" content="text/html; charset=utf-8" />
</head>
<body>
<h1 xml:lang="en">Welcome to our Website</h1>
<p xml:lang="en">This website offers a variety of products.</p>
```

```
<h1 xml:lang="fr">Bienvenue sur notre site web</h1>
<p xml:lang="fr">Ce site web propose une variété de produits.</p>
</body>
</html>
```

Implementing a Cookie Consent Banner

```
<!DOCTYPE html PUBLIC "-//W3C//DTD XHTML 1.0 Strict//EN"
    "http://www.w3.org/TR/xhtml1/DTD/xhtml1-strict.dtd">
<html xmlns="http://www.w3.org/1999/xhtml" xml:lang="en" lang="en">
<head>
  <title>Implementing a Cookie Consent Banner</title>
  <meta http-equiv="Content-Type" content="text/html; charset=utf-8" />
  <style type="text/css">
    .cookie-banner {
      position: fixed;
      bottom: 0;
      left: 0;
      width: 100%;
      background-color: #333;
      color: #fff;
      padding: 10px 20px;
      text-align: center;
      font-size: 14px;
    }
    .cookie-banner button {
      background-color: #4CAF50;
      color: white;
      border: none;
```

```
      padding: 10px 20px;

      text-align: center;

      text-decoration: none;

      display: inline-block;

      font-size: 14px;

      margin-left: 10px;

      cursor: pointer;

    }

    .cookie-banner button:hover {

      background-color: #45a049;

    }

  </style>

</head>

<body>

<div class="cookie-banner">

  This website uses cookies. <button

onclick="acceptCookies()">Accept</button>

</div>

<script type="text/javascript">

  function acceptCookies() {

    // Set cookie or any other action on acceptance

    // For simplicity, we hide the banner here

    document.querySelector('.cookie-banner').style.display = 'none';

  }

</script>

</body>

</html>
```

Creating a Responsive Pricing Table

```
<!DOCTYPE html PUBLIC "-//W3C//DTD XHTML 1.0 Strict//EN"
    "http://www.w3.org/TR/xhtml1/DTD/xhtml1-strict.dtd">
<html xmlns="http://www.w3.org/1999/xhtml" xml:lang="en" lang="en">
<head>
  <title>Creating a Responsive Pricing Table</title>
  <meta http-equiv="Content-Type" content="text/html; charset=utf-8" />
  <style type="text/css">
    .pricing-table {
      width: 100%;
      max-width: 800px;
      margin: 20px auto;
      border-collapse: collapse;
      text-align: center;
    }
    .pricing-table th, .pricing-table td {
      padding: 15px;
      border: 1px solid #ccc;
    }
    .pricing-table th {
      background-color: #f0f0f0;
    }
    .pricing-table .highlight {
      background-color: #4CAF50;
      color: white;
    }
    .pricing-table .highlight td {
      background-color: #f0f0f0;
```

```
        font-weight: bold;
      }
      @media only screen and (max-width: 600px) {
        .pricing-table {
          font-size: 14px;
        }
      }
    </style>
  </head>
  <body>
  <table class="pricing-table">
    <tr>
      <th>Plan</th>
      <th>Features</th>
      <th>Price</th>
    </tr>
    <tr>
      <td>Basic</td>
      <td>Feature 1, Feature 2</td>
      <td>$9.99/month</td>
    </tr>
    <tr class="highlight">
      <td>Pro</td>
      <td>Feature 1, Feature 2, Feature 3</td>
      <td>$19.99/month</td>
    </tr>
    <tr>
      <td>Enterprise</td>
```

```
      <td>Feature 1, Feature 2, Feature 3, Feature 4</td>
      <td>$49.99/month</td>
   </tr>
</table>
</body>
</html>
```

Using XHTML for Semantic Markup (Semantic Elements)

```
<!DOCTYPE html PUBLIC "-//W3C//DTD XHTML 1.0 Strict//EN"
     "http://www.w3.org/TR/xhtml1/DTD/xhtml1-strict.dtd">
<html xmlns="http://www.w3.org/1999/xhtml" xml:lang="en" lang="en">
<head>
  <title>Using XHTML for Semantic Markup (Semantic Elements)</title>
  <meta http-equiv="Content-Type" content="text/html; charset=utf-8" />
  <style type="text/css">
    article {
      border: 1px solid #ccc;
      padding: 10px;
      margin-bottom: 20px;
    }
    section {
      margin-bottom: 10px;
    }
    aside {
      float: right;
      width: 30%;
      margin-left: 10px;
      background-color: #f0f0f0;
```

```
      padding: 10px;
    }
    footer {
      clear: both;
      background-color: #333;
      color: #fff;
      text-align: center;
      padding: 10px;
    }
  </style>
</head>
<body>
<article>
  <header>
    <h1>Article Title</h1>
  </header>
  <section>
    <p>Main content goes here.</p>
  </section>
  <aside>
    <h2>Related Links</h2>
    <ul>
      <li><a href="#">Link 1</a></li>
      <li><a href="#">Link 2</a></li>
      <li><a href="#">Link 3</a></li>
    </ul>
  </aside>
  <footer>
```

© 2024 Your Website. All Rights Reserved.

```
    </footer>
  </article>
</body>
</html>
```

Implementing a Hover Effect with Image Overlays

```
<!DOCTYPE html PUBLIC "-//W3C//DTD XHTML 1.0 Strict//EN"
    "http://www.w3.org/TR/xhtml1/DTD/xhtml1-strict.dtd">
<html xmlns="http://www.w3.org/1999/xhtml" xml:lang="en" lang="en">
<head>
  <title>Implementing a Hover Effect with Image Overlays</title>
  <meta http-equiv="Content-Type" content="text/html; charset=utf-8" />
  <style type="text/css">
    .image-container {
      position: relative;
      width: 300px;
      height: 200px;
      overflow: hidden;
    }
    .image {
      width: 100%;
      height: 100%;
      transition: transform 0.3s ease;
    }
    .overlay {
      position: absolute;
      top: 0;
```

```
        left: 0;

        width: 100%;

        height: 100%;

        background-color: rgba(0, 0, 0, 0.5);

        color: #fff;

        display: flex;

        justify-content: center;

        align-items: center;

        opacity: 0;

        transition: opacity 0.3s ease;

    }

    .image-container:hover .overlay {

        opacity: 1;

    }

    .text {

        text-align: center;

        font-size: 24px;

    }

    </style>

</head>

<body>

<div class="image-container">

    <img src="image.jpg" alt="Image" class="image" />

    <div class="overlay">

        <div class="text">View Details</div>

    </div>

</div>

</body>
```

```
</html>
```

Creating a Progress Indicator for Form Submission

```html
<!DOCTYPE html PUBLIC "-//W3C//DTD XHTML 1.0 Strict//EN"
    "http://www.w3.org/TR/xhtml1/DTD/xhtml1-strict.dtd">
<html xmlns="http://www.w3.org/1999/xhtml" xml:lang="en" lang="en">
<head>
  <title>Creating a Progress Indicator for Form Submission</title>
  <meta http-equiv="Content-Type" content="text/html; charset=utf-8" />
  <style type="text/css">
    .form-container {
      width: 300px;
      margin: 20px auto;
    }
    .form-group {
      margin-bottom: 10px;
    }
    .form-group label {
      display: block;
      margin-bottom: 5px;
    }
    .form-group input {
      width: 100%;
      padding: 5px;
      font-size: 14px;
    }
    .submit-btn {
      display: block;
```

```
      width: 100%;

      padding: 10px;

      background-color: #333;

      color: #fff;

      border: none;

      cursor: pointer;

    }

    .submit-btn:hover {

      background-color: #555;

    }

    .progress {

      width: 100%;

      height: 20px;

      background-color: #f0f0f0;

      margin-top: 10px;

      display: none;

    }

    .progress-bar {

      width: 0;

      height: 100%;

      background-color: #4CAF50;

    }

  </style>

</head>

<body>

<div class="form-container">

  <form id="submitForm" action="#" method="post"

onsubmit="submitForm(event)">
```

```
      <div class="form-group">
        <label for="name">Name:</label>
        <input type="text" id="name" name="name" required />
      </div>
      <div class="form-group">
        <label for="email">Email:</label>
        <input type="email" id="email" name="email" required />
      </div>
      <button type="submit" class="submit-btn">Submit</button>
      <div class="progress">
        <div class="progress-bar" id="progressBar"></div>
      </div>
    </form>
  </div>
  <script type="text/javascript">
    function submitForm(event) {
      event.preventDefault();
      var progressBar = document.getElementById('progressBar');
      var progress = 0;
      var interval = setInterval(function() {
        progress += 10;
        progressBar.style.width = progress + '%';
        if (progress >= 100) {
          clearInterval(interval);
          // Simulate form submission completion
          setTimeout(function() {
            document.getElementById('submitForm').submit();
          }, 500);
```

```
      }
    }, 100);
  }
</script>
</body>
</html>
```

Implementing a "Read More" Button for Expanding Text

```
<!DOCTYPE html PUBLIC "-//W3C//DTD XHTML 1.0 Strict//EN"
    "http://www.w3.org/TR/xhtml1/DTD/xhtml1-strict.dtd">
<html xmlns="http://www.w3.org/1999/xhtml" xml:lang="en" lang="en">
<head>
  <title>Implementing a "Read More" Button for Expanding Text</title>
  <meta http-equiv="Content-Type" content="text/html; charset=utf-8" />
  <style type="text/css">
    .content {
      max-height: 100px;
      overflow: hidden;
      transition: max-height 0.3s ease;
    }
    .expanded {
      max-height: none;
    }
    .read-more-btn {
      display: inline-block;
      background-color: #333;
      color: #fff;
      padding: 5px 10px;
```

```
    text-decoration: none;
      cursor: pointer;
    }
  </style>
</head>
<body>
<div id="content" class="content">
    <p>Lorem ipsum dolor sit amet, consectetur adipiscing elit. Nulla convallis
libero non nunc iaculis aliquam.</p>
    <p>Phasellus consequat neque nec ligula commodo interdum. Vivamus
eleifend, odio sed gravida commodo.</p>
</div>
<a href="#" id="readMoreBtn" class="read-more-btn"
onclick="toggleReadMore(event)">Read More</a>
<script type="text/javascript">
    function toggleReadMore(event) {
      event.preventDefault();
      var content = document.getElementById('content');
      var readMoreBtn = document.getElementById('readMoreBtn');
      if (content.classList.contains('expanded')) {
        content.classList.remove('expanded');
        readMoreBtn.textContent = 'Read More';
      } else {
        content.classList.add('expanded');
        readMoreBtn.textContent = 'Show Less';
      }
    }
</script>
```

```
</body>
</html>
```

Using XHTML for SEO Optimization (Meta Tags, Structured Data)

```
<!DOCTYPE html PUBLIC "-//W3C//DTD XHTML 1.0 Strict//EN"
    "http://www.w3.org/TR/xhtml1/DTD/xhtml1-strict.dtd">
<html xmlns="http://www.w3.org/1999/xhtml" xml:lang="en" lang="en">
<head>
  <title>Using XHTML for SEO Optimization (Meta Tags, Structured
Data)</title>
  <meta http-equiv="Content-Type" content="text/html; charset=utf-8" />
  <meta name="description" content="This is an example of XHTML page
optimized for SEO." />
  <meta name="keywords" content="XHTML, SEO, meta tags, structured data"
/>
  <meta name="author" content="Your Name" />
  <meta name="robots" content="index, follow" />
  <script type="application/ld+json">
    {
      "@context": "http://schema.org",
      "@type": "Organization",
      "name": "Your Website",
      "url": "http://www.yourwebsite.com",
      "logo": "http://www.yourwebsite.com/logo.png",
      "contactPoint": {
        "@type": "ContactPoint",
        "telephone": "+1-123-456-7890",
        "contactType": "Customer Service",
```

```
      "contactOption": "TollFree",

      "areaServed": "US",

      "availableLanguage": ["English", "Spanish"]

    },

    "sameAs": [

      "http://www.facebook.com/yourwebsite",

      "http://www.twitter.com/yourwebsite",

      "http://plus.google.com/+yourwebsite"

    ]

   }

  </script>

</head>

<body>

<h1>Main Content Title</h1>

<p>Main content goes here.</p>

</body>

</html>
```

Implementing Drag-and-Drop Functionality

```
<!DOCTYPE html PUBLIC "-//W3C//DTD XHTML 1.0 Strict//EN"

    "http://www.w3.org/TR/xhtml1/DTD/xhtml1-strict.dtd">

<html xmlns="http://www.w3.org/1999/xhtml" xml:lang="en" lang="en">

<head>

  <title>Implementing Drag-and-Drop Functionality</title>

  <meta http-equiv="Content-Type" content="text/html; charset=utf-8" />

  <style type="text/css">

    .drag-container {

      width: 300px;
```

```
      height: 200px;

      border: 2px dashed #ccc;

      text-align: center;

      line-height: 200px;

      cursor: pointer;

    }

    .dropped {

      background-color: #f0f0f0;

    }

  </style>

</head>

<body>

<div id="dragContainer" class="drag-container" draggable="true"

ondragstart="dragStart(event)">

  Drag Me!

</div>

<div id="dropContainer" class="drag-container" ondragover="dragOver(event)"

ondrop="drop(event)">

  Drop Here!

</div>

<script type="text/javascript">

  function dragStart(event) {

    event.dataTransfer.setData("text", event.target.id);

  }

  function dragOver(event) {

    event.preventDefault();

  }

  function drop(event) {
```

```
      event.preventDefault();

      var data = event.dataTransfer.getData("text");

      var draggedElement = document.getElementById(data);

      var dropContainer = document.getElementById('dropContainer');

      if (!dropContainer.classList.contains('dropped')) {

        dropContainer.classList.add('dropped');

        dropContainer.innerHTML = 'Dropped!';

      }

    }

</script>

</body>

</html>
```

Creating a Sidebar Navigation Menu with Collapsible Sections

```
<!DOCTYPE html PUBLIC "-//W3C//DTD XHTML 1.0 Strict//EN"
    "http://www.w3.org/TR/xhtml1/DTD/xhtml1-strict.dtd">
<html xmlns="http://www.w3.org/1999/xhtml" xml:lang="en" lang="en">
<head>
  <title>Creating a Sidebar Navigation Menu with Collapsible Sections</title>
  <meta http-equiv="Content-Type" content="text/html; charset=utf-8" />
  <style type="text/css">
    body {
      font-family: Arial, sans-serif;
      margin: 0;
      padding: 0;
      display: flex;
    }
    .sidebar {
```

```
      width: 250px;

      background-color: #333;

      color: #fff;

      padding: 20px;

      box-sizing: border-box;

    }

    .sidebar h2 {

      margin-top: 0;

      cursor: pointer;

    }

    .menu-item {

      margin-bottom: 10px;

    }

    .sub-menu {

      display: none;

      padding-left: 20px;

    }

    .sub-menu a {

      color: #ccc;

      text-decoration: none;

    }

    .sub-menu a:hover {

      color: #fff;

    }

  </style>

</head>

<body>

<div class="sidebar">
```

```html
    <h2 onclick="toggleSubMenu('section1')">Section 1</h2>
    <ul id="section1" class="sub-menu">
      <li class="menu-item"><a href="#">Sub Item 1.1</a></li>
      <li class="menu-item"><a href="#">Sub Item 1.2</a></li>
      <li class="menu-item"><a href="#">Sub Item 1.3</a></li>
    </ul>
    <h2 onclick="toggleSubMenu('section2')">Section 2</h2>
    <ul id="section2" class="sub-menu">
      <li class="menu-item"><a href="#">Sub Item 2.1</a></li>
      <li class="menu-item"><a href="#">Sub Item 2.2</a></li>
    </ul>
  </div>
  <div class="content">
    <!-- Main content goes here -->
  </div>
  <script type="text/javascript">
    function toggleSubMenu(sectionId) {
      var section = document.getElementById(sectionId);
      if (section.style.display === 'block') {
        section.style.display = 'none';
      } else {
        section.style.display = 'block';
      }
    }
  </script>
</body>
</html>
```

Using XHTML for Responsive Typography (Viewport Units, Fluid Typography)

```
<!DOCTYPE html PUBLIC "-//W3C//DTD XHTML 1.0 Strict//EN"
    "http://www.w3.org/TR/xhtml1/DTD/xhtml1-strict.dtd">
<html xmlns="http://www.w3.org/1999/xhtml" xml:lang="en" lang="en">
<head>
  <title>Using XHTML for Responsive Typography (Viewport Units, Fluid
Typography)</title>
  <meta http-equiv="Content-Type" content="text/html; charset=utf-8" />
  <style type="text/css">
    body {
        font-family: Arial, sans-serif;
        margin: 0;
        padding: 0;
        display: flex;
        justify-content: center;
        align-items: center;
        height: 100vh;
        text-align: center;
    }
    .heading {
        font-size: 6vw; /* Responsive font size based on viewport width */
        margin-bottom: 20px;
    }
    .paragraph {
        font-size: 4vw;
        line-height: 1.5;
    }
```

```
    </style>
</head>
<body>
<h1 class="heading">Responsive Typography Example</h1>
<p class="paragraph">Lorem ipsum dolor sit amet, consectetur adipiscing elit.
Nullam placerat mauris at placerat vehicula.</p>
</body>
</html>
```

Implementing Keyboard Navigation for Accessibility

```
<!DOCTYPE html PUBLIC "-//W3C//DTD XHTML 1.0 Strict//EN"
    "http://www.w3.org/TR/xhtml1/DTD/xhtml1-strict.dtd">
<html xmlns="http://www.w3.org/1999/xhtml" xml:lang="en" lang="en">
<head>
  <title>Implementing Keyboard Navigation for Accessibility</title>
  <meta http-equiv="Content-Type" content="text/html; charset=utf-8" />
  <style type="text/css">
    body {
      font-family: Arial, sans-serif;
      margin: 0;
      padding: 0;
    }
    .nav-container {
      width: 100%;
      background-color: #333;
      color: #fff;
      padding: 10px 20px;
      box-sizing: border-box;
```

```
      }
      .nav-list {
         list-style-type: none;
         padding: 0;
         margin: 0;
         display: flex;
         justify-content: center;
      }
      .nav-item {
         margin: 0 10px;
      }
      .nav-link {
         color: #fff;
         text-decoration: none;
         cursor: pointer;
         padding: 5px 10px;
      }
      .nav-link:hover {
         background-color: #555;
      }
   </style>
</head>
<body>
<div class="nav-container">
   <ul class="nav-list">
      <li class="nav-item"><a href="#" class="nav-link"
onclick="navigate(event, 'home')">Home</a></li>
```

```
      <li class="nav-item"><a href="#" class="nav-link"
onclick="navigate(event, 'about')">About</a></li>
      <li class="nav-item"><a href="#" class="nav-link"
onclick="navigate(event, 'services')">Services</a></li>
      <li class="nav-item"><a href="#" class="nav-link"
onclick="navigate(event, 'contact')">Contact</a></li>
   </ul>
</div>
<div id="content">
   <!-- Main content goes here -->
</div>
<script type="text/javascript">
   function navigate(event, sectionId) {
      event.preventDefault();
      var content = document.getElementById('content');
      content.textContent = 'Navigated to ' + sectionId + ' section.';
   }
</script>
</body>
</html>
```